# Language for Study

## LEVEL 1

Tamsin Espinosa   Claire Henstock   Clare Walsh

Series editor: Ian Smallwood

**CAMBRIDGE**

CAMBRIDGE UNIVERSITY PRESS
Cambridge, New York, Melbourne, Madrid, Cape Town,
Singapore, São Paulo, Delhi, Mexico City

Cambridge University Press
The Edinburgh Building, Cambridge CB2 8RU, UK

www.cambridge.org
Information on this title: www.cambridge.org/9781107689190

First published 2012

Printed and bound in the United Kingdom by the MPG Books Group

*A catalogue record for this publication is available from the British Library*

ISBN 978-1-107-68919-0

Cambridge University Press has no responsibility for the persistence or
accuracy of URLs for external or third-party internet websites referred to in
this publication, and does not guarantee that any content on such websites is,
or will remain, accurate or appropriate. Information regarding prices, travel
timetables and other factual information given in this work is correct at
the time of first printing but Cambridge University Press does not guarantee
the accuracy of such information thereafter.

**Acknowledgments**
The authors and publishers acknowledge the following sources of
copyright material and are grateful for the permissions granted.
While every effort has been made, it has not always been possible
to identify the sources of all the material used, or to trace all
copyright holders. If any omissions are brought to our notice, we
will be happy to include the appropriate acknowledgements on
reprinting.

Loughborough University for the text on p.14 'Deep and surface
approaches to learning', adapted from: Houghton, W. (2004).
*Engineering Subject Centre Guide: Learning and Teaching Theory
for Engineering Academics*. Loughborough University: HEA
Engineering Subject Centre. Reproduced with permission; Dr
Sonia Livingstone, London School of Economics and Political
Science for the text on p.72–73 'How children use the media'
based on Young People, New Media, Summary of Report of the
Research Project. Children, Young People and the Changing
Media Environment. Reproduced with permission; World
Wind Energy Association for the chart on p.140, adapted
from The World Wind Energy Report, 2010. www.wwindea.
org. Reproduced with permission; GreenSpec for the diagrams
on p.141 from the website www.greenspec.co.uk/small-wind-
turbines. php. Reproduced with permission., www.greenspec.
co.uk; United Nations Statistics Division for the graph on p.144.
Copyright © United Nations Statistics Division (2011). Retrieved
from: http://data.un.org/Data.aspx?q = + greenhouse + gas&
d = GHG&f = seriesID%3aGHG. Reproduced with permission;
Organisation for Economic Co-operation and Development for
the graph on p.145. Information retrieved from OECD (2010),
"Renewable Energy", in *OECD Factbook 2010: Economic,*

*Environmental and Social Statistics*, OECD Publishing,
http://dx.doi.org/10.1787/factbook-2010-41-en. Reproduced with
permission.

**Photo acknowledgments**
p.4 1 ©Chris Schmidt/istockphoto.com, p.4 2 ©Muharrem Öner/
istockphoto.com, p.4 3 ©Fernando Alonso Herrero/istockphoto.
com, p.4 4 ©Image Source/Getty images;
p.6 ©Chris Schmidt/istockphoto.com; p.54 ©Muharrem Öner/
istockphoto.com; p.101 ©Fernando Alonso Herrero/istockphoto.
com; p.121 t ©The Power of Forever Photography/istockphotos.
com, b ©Nabi Lukic/istockphotos.com; p.160 ©Getty images

**Author acknowledgments**
The authoring team would like to thank Clare Sheridan, Ian
Morrison, Nick Robinson, Nik White, Andrew Jurascheck, Chris
Capper and Ian Collier for their help and support. They offer
grateful acknowledgment to Sarah Clark, Fred Gooch, and Neil
McSweeney for their advice and contributions to the manuscripts.
They would also like to thank all ELT and academic skills staff
and students across Kaplan International Colleges for their
assistance in trialling the materials during development and for
their valuable feedback and suggestions.

**Publisher acknowledgments**
The authors and publishers would like to thank the following
people who reviewed and commented on the material at various
stages: Olwyn Alexander, Michael
McCarthy, Jenifer Spencer, and Scott Thornbury

Design and illustrations by Hart McLeod, Cambridge

# Language for study Contents

# Map of the book

| | **Part A** Understanding spoken information | **Part B** Understanding written information |
|---|---|---|
| **1** **Approaches to learning**  | Understanding the use of stress in sentences<br>Developing strategies for learning vocabulary<br>Understanding modals | Recognizing different word forms<br>Understanding the language of comparison |
|  **LESSON TASK** | **Assessing strategies for improving academic vocabulary** | **Comparing texts and information** |
| **2** **Communication**  | Using rising and falling intonation<br>Using pauses to improve comprehension<br>Preparing for lectures by predicting vocabulary | Understanding how comment adverbs indicate degrees of certainty<br>Recognizing how modal auxiliary verbs indicate certainty<br>Using adverbs of degree to emphasize meaning |
|  **LESSON TASK** | **Listening for intonation and pauses** | **Expressing opinions** |
| **3** **Science and technology in society**  | Noticing signpost words and phrases<br>Predicting and identifying key words in context<br>Identifying cause and effect linking words and arguments | Identifying key vocabulary<br>Using prepositional phrases<br>Expressing possibility |
| **LESSON TASK** | **Developing arguments in speaking** | **Reading critically** |
| **4** **Health issues** | Understanding how linking words signpost an argument<br>Understanding how discourse markers signpost an argument | Using modifiers with comparatives and superlatives<br>Paraphrasing using words with an opposite meaning<br>Understanding how commas improve clarity |
|  **LESSON TASK** | **Using linking words and discourse markers** | **Improving the clarity of your writing** |

| Part C<br>Investigating | Part D<br>Reporting in speech | Part E<br>Reporting in writing |
|---|---|---|
| Identifying and using collocations<br>Using relative clauses to include essential information in sentences<br>Using relative clauses to include non-essential information in sentences | Recognizing and using the language of academic discussions<br>Referring to other people's ideas in discussion | Understanding general features of academic writing<br>Stating aims in a formal register<br>Using compound nouns |
| **Describing features of academic work** | **Conducting an effective discussion** | **Writing in a formal register** |
| Using questions to encourage participation<br>Checking understanding<br>Choosing between Past Simple and Present Perfect Simple | Using rhetorical questions<br>Using the phonemic alphabet | Referring to an author's work<br>Using the Active or Passive to paraphrase<br>Changing word forms and using synonyms to paraphrase |
| **Working in a group** | **Giving a short presentation** | **Paraphrasing information** |
| Recognizing your reading level<br>Using synonyms<br>Understanding substitution | Using signpost words and phrases in presentations<br>Dealing with questions<br>Using intonation to maintain interest<br>Referring to visual materials | Reporting ideas from sources<br>Summarizing information from other sources<br>Integrating information from sources into writing |
| **Following academic sources** | **Giving a presentation with visuals** | **Summarizing and reporting information** |
| Making efficient notes<br>Using discourse markers to understand abstracts<br>Understanding written discourse markers | Expressing the aims of a presentation using clauses of purpose<br>Understanding differences between spoken and written academic English<br>Understanding and using connected speech | Showing your position using adverbs and adjectives<br>Making recommendations and giving warnings in conclusions<br>Developing your writing style by varying the length of your sentences |
| **Using abstracts to locate academic sources** | **Introducing a presentation** | **Reviewing proofreading skills** |

# Unit 1 Approaches to learning

## Unit overview

| Part | This part will help you to … | By improving your ability to … |
|------|------------------------------|--------------------------------|
| A | **Follow lectures** | • understand the use of stress in sentences<br>• develop strategies for learning vocabulary<br>• understand modals. |
| B | **Understand and compare academic texts** | • recognize different word forms<br>• understand the language of comparison. |
| C | **Research academic texts** | • identify and use collocations<br>• use relative clauses to include essential information in sentences<br>• use relative clauses to include non-essential information in sentences. |
| D | **Participate in tutorials** | • recognize and use the language of academic discussions<br>• refer to other people's ideas in discussion. |
| E | **Write an essay** | • understand general features of academic writing<br>• use compound nouns<br>• write in a formal register. |

# Understanding spoken information

**By the end of Part A you will be able to:**

- understand the use of stress in sentences
- develop strategies for learning vocabulary
- understand modals.

Developing effective listening skills is essential for successful tertiary study. However, many students find listening difficult. You are often told to 'practise more' – and this will help, but only if you can understand what you are listening to! Throughout this course, you will be helped to develop a range of strategies and techniques to improve your listening.

## 1 Understanding the use of stress in sentences

**1a** You are going to listen to an extract from a lecture giving suggestions on how to improve your understanding of lectures in English. Work in pairs. Discuss what you think some of the suggestions might be. Write your ideas below.

---
**Suggestions for improving listening skills in lectures**
---

**1b** Listen to the extract and check your ideas in 1a. Add any more suggestions you hear.

1.1

**1c** Listen to the first part of the extract again. Underline any words in the sentences (1–4) which are emphasized or stressed more than others.

**1** But why is it that people think listening to a lecture is such hard work when, for example, listening to a friend is easy and, usually, enjoyable?

**2** Well, one thing you might think about is the difference between hearing and listening.

**3** Simply hearing is what your ears do – your brain doesn't have to make any conscious effort to think about what is being heard.

**4** But listening, well that's what you do when you're interested, when you have a purpose or a need for the information.

**1d** Compare your answers with a partner. Discuss why some words are stressed more than others. How might listening for stressed words help you in lectures?

### Content and function words

> Words which provide the essential meaning of a sentence are called *content* words. In spoken English, these words are often stressed. Words which are grammatically necessary but which do not carry meaning are called *function* words. These words are not usually stressed, except for special emphasis. Examples of content and function words are given in the table below.

**1e**   Work in pairs. Add more examples from the sentences in 1c to each category.

| Content words (usually stressed) | Function words (usually unstressed) |
|---|---|
| **Nouns:**<br>*discussion, essay, lecture* | **Pronouns:**<br>*we, they, anybody, one* |
| **Adjectives:**<br>*interesting, academic, scientific* | **Prepositions:**<br>*in, of, at, between* |
| **Verbs:**<br>*listen, study, hear, lecture* | **Auxiliary verbs:**<br>*be, have* |
| **Adverbs:**<br>*really, very, also, enough* | **Conjunctions:**<br>*and, or, when, while* |
| | **Articles:**<br>*a, an* |

**1f**   Read this extract from a different talk on listening to lectures. Do you agree with the advice?

> Firstly, think about what you can do to get more from lectures yourself. Prepare your mind by reading and thinking about the topic before the lecture. Then, during the lecture, don't try to note down everything you hear like a dictation exercise, but make a note of key points and think about how they relate to the things you already know. Consider which key points you want – or need – to follow up by yourself.

**1g**   Based on the table in 1e, underline the content words in the extract in 1f.

**1h**   Listen to the extract and check whether the words you underlined are stressed.

1.2

> Remember that a speaker can use additional word stress on both content or function words (and/or sometimes a pause) to reinforce a main point. For example, the speaker in the first extract you listened to stressed the words *hearing* and *listening* more than any other words in order to emphasize the difference between the two actions.

> **Example**
> *Well, one thing you might think about is the difference between* **hearing** *and* **listening**.
>
> Stressing certain words more than others helps to ensure that the listener understands the most important words. This frequently happens when comparing or contrasting two words.

**1i** Read the introduction to a lecture on different approaches to learning. Underline the content words, then draw a circle around any words that might require additional stress.

> Have you ever wondered what it is that makes a student successful? Is it the amount of work that the student does, or the way that they do it? Does it depend on the teacher? Can a good teacher really make students perform better, or does it all come down to what's going on inside the student's mind during the learning process? Is it a combination of these? Today I'm going to introduce the idea of 'approaches to learning'; the notion that different students take different approaches to the way they study and how this is likely to affect their long-term success.

1.3

**1j** Listen to the extract and check your answers. Which words does the speaker give added stress to?

## 2 Developing strategies for learning vocabulary

> Your ability to understand a lecture will increase if you are familiar with the vocabulary the lecturer uses. During this course, you will be introduced to vocabulary which is regularly used in academic contexts. You should make sure you can understand and use as much of this vocabulary as possible. Everybody has their own way of increasing their vocabulary, so you should develop your own strategies for recording, learning and revising new words.

**2a** Work in groups. Find out which strategies for developing vocabulary the other students already use and discuss how these strategies work.

1.4

**2b** Listen to the first part of a lecture on strategies for learning vocabulary. The speaker suggests there are four questions you should ask yourself when considering what strategy to use. Write them below.

| Strategies for learning vocabulary |
| --- |
| 1 |
| 2 |

```
3


4
```

1.5

**2c** Listen to the rest of the lecture. Under each question in 2b, make notes on the speaker's main suggestions.

**2d** Read the transcript of the lecture in **Appendix 1** and check your answers.

**2e** Work in pairs. Look at the words in this box, which are from the lecture. Identify the form of each word (e.g. noun, verb, etc.), then discuss what each word means.

| focus | context | specific | discipline | categories | purposes |
|-------|---------|----------|------------|------------|----------|

**2f** Choose three of the words from the box above. Write a sentence on 'strategies for learning vocabulary' for each word.

***Example***
*It's a good idea to make separate lists of vocabulary for general academic vocabulary and for vocabulary which is **specific** to your subject.*

**2g** Work in small groups. Take turns to read your sentences aloud without saying the words you chose in 2f. Your group guesses the missing words.

***Example***

> It's a good idea to make separate lists of vocabulary for general academic vocabulary and for vocabulary which is _____ to your subject.

> Is it 'specific'?

> Yes, that's right.

## 3 Understanding modals

**3a** Read this extract from the lecture you heard in 2b. What is the purpose of the lecture: give an order, make a request, or give advice?

Perhaps you **could** make separate lists for words you feel you are likely to come across in a general academic context, and those you feel are more specific to your own discipline or are more technical in nature. You **might** also try to place the words into different categories, according to how or where they are most likely to be used. You **should** be refining these categories constantly as your records increase.

Of course, to be able to do this properly, you **must** first decide what you mean by 'a word'. You should always consider the different forms in a word family and group these together. For example, if you come across the word *analyze*, you **need to** explore what other forms of the word might be used in different contexts – words such as *analysis*, *analytical* or *analytically* and even *analyst*. You **should** make sure you are familiar with them all and can use them all correctly.

**3b** Work in pairs. Discuss the differences in meaning between the words in bold in the text.

*Example*
*Could* is used to give suggestions, whereas *should* is used to give stronger recommendations.

> *Could*, *might*, *should* and *must* are modals.
>
> Modals and *need to* are commonly used when making suggestions or recommendations to indicate the 'force' of the suggestion.
>
> A modal is an auxiliary verb that does not change and is used with the base form of the verb.
>
> *Examples*
> *There are a few basic questions which you* ***should*** *consider while you design your strategy.*
>
> *You* ***must*** *first decide what you mean by 'a word'.*

**3c** One of the examples in the information box above is more 'forceful' than the other. Work in pairs. Look at the transcript in 3a and write each word in bold in the appropriate position on the line below (some modals may be of approximately equal 'force').

**Most force**                                                                 **Least force**

*should*

**3d** Look at the notes you made in 2c. Choose five suggestions which were made during the lecture. Write a sentence for each one, using a different modal in each sentence to reflect how strongly you feel the suggestions should be followed.

*Example*
*You* ***should*** *record the pronunciation of a word, as well as the meaning and spelling.*

1

2

3

4

5

**3e** Work in pairs. Compare your suggestions and discuss any differences in the content of the suggestion or the modal you have used. Explain your reasons for choosing the modal with a particular force.

> **LESSON TASK** **4 Assessing strategies for improving academic vocabulary**

**4a** Work in small groups. Write down the best strategies for recording, learning and revising new academic vocabulary.

**4b** Present your suggestions to the rest of the class and explain why you think they are a good way of increasing your academic vocabulary.

**4c** While you listen to other groups outlining their strategies, write down any ideas you think are useful.

**4d** Work in small groups. Decide which are the three best strategies and why.

## 5 Review and extension

### Vocabulary consolidation

**5a** Complete this table with the missing word forms. Use a dictionary to help you if necessary.

| Noun | Verb | Adjective |
|---|---|---|
| | participate | |
| | emphasize | |
| category | | |
| | identify | |
| strategy | | |
| | formulate | |
| | require | |
| | | specific |
| concentration | | |
| | substitute | – |

**5b** Choose five words from the table and use them in sentences of your own which make recommendations about approaches to study. Use a different modal in each sentence to reflect how strongly you feel about your recommendation. Write your sentences in the box on p.13.

*Example*
*You must **participate** in discussions in class.*

| | |
|---|---|
| **1** | |
| **2** | |
| **3** | |
| **4** | |
| **5** | |

**Syllable stress**

1.6

**5c** In English, the main stress is placed on one syllable in each word. Most two-syllable nouns and adjectives place stress on the first syllable. Most two-syllable verbs place stress on the second syllable. Listen to these words and mark the stressed syllables.

| | | | | | |
|---|---|---|---|---|---|
| **1** lecture | | **2** easy | | **3** instruct | |
| **4** reflect | | **5** import | | **6** clever | |
| **7** decide | | **8** import | | | |

**5d** Look again at the two forms of *import*. Which is a noun and which is a verb?

**5e** Look at the sentences you wrote in 5b. Practise reading each sentence aloud, making sure you use syllable and word stress accurately.

**Developing a personal vocabulary logbook**

**5f** It is important to design and use a personal vocabulary logbook to enable you to record and learn new vocabulary. Start by deciding how you are going to organize your logbook and then consider which vocabulary items in this unit you should include in it. Think about how you are going to use your logbook: how are you going to remember and practise the items in it?

# Understanding written information

**By the end of Part B you will be able to:**
- recognize different word forms
- understand the language of comparison.

## 1 Recognizing different word forms

**1a** You are going to read a short text comparing two approaches to learning – *deep learning* and *surface learning*. Work in groups. Discuss what you think the two terms mean and how they are different.

**1b** Compare your answers with other groups.

**1c** Read the text below. Write notes on features of the different types of learning.

| Deep learning | Surface learning |
| --- | --- |
| | |

Simply stated, *deep learning* involves the critical analysis of new ideas, linking them to already-known concepts and principles, and leads to understanding and long-term retention of ideas so that they can be used for problem solving in unfamiliar contexts. Deep learning promotes understanding and application for life. In contrast, *surface learning* is a more superficial acceptance of information and memorization as isolated and unlinked facts. It leads to short-term retention of material for examinations and does not promote understanding or long-term retention of knowledge and information.

Critical to our understanding of this principle is that we should not identify the student with a fixed approach to learning, but it is the design of the learning opportunity that encourages students to adopt a particular approach. We need to analyze the way we are teaching and identify the most likely methodology to encourage deep learning.

**1d** Work in groups. Discuss these questions.

  1 Who is the text written for?

  2 Do you agree with the advice in the second paragraph? Explain your reasons.

**1e** Work in pairs. Decide whether the words in bold in these extracts from academic sources are verbs, nouns or adjectives. Write them in the correct column in the table below. Then complete the other columns.

1 These students were **identified** with adopting a deep approach to learning.

2 The main **identifying** characteristic of this type of learner is the ability to apply what they have learned to different contexts.

3 The second group tried to remember facts contained within the text, **identifying** and focusing on what they thought they would be asked later.

4 The main aim of the article is to **identify** the two approaches to learning and to suggest ways in which educators might encourage the more effective approach.

5 Barnett, for instance, **defines** a student as 'someone who … throws herself into her studies' (Barnett, 2007, p.18).

6 This has led to the **definition** of teaching as enabling student learning.

| Verb | Noun | Adjective |
| --- | --- | --- |
| | *analysis* | |
| | | |
| | | |
| | | |

**1f** Check your answers with a partner.

**1g** Read the paragraph below and write the words in bold in the correct column of the table in 1e. Then complete the other columns.

Research shows clear differences in the defining **characteristics** of student approaches to learning. However, it would be a mistake to characterize any student as taking a deep or surface approach all the time. Instead, it is more likely that students tend to adopt **different** approaches in different contexts. A simple **distinction**, therefore, between deep and surface learners is not necessarily an accurate picture of student learning styles. The most **successful** students are likely to be those who take a blended approach, and combine the positive aspects of surface approaches (memorization when necessary, and goal focus) with the interest and **engagement** in a subject that is **typical** of the deep approach.

**1h** Choose two rows from the table in 1e. Write a sentence for the three forms of each word, illustrating their different uses.

*Example*
*One of the key **characteristics** of a successful learner is the ability to work hard.*
*Surface learners are **characterized** by a focus on exams and a shallower understanding of the topic.*
*Success in the classroom depends, to an extent, on the **character** of the learner.*

1a

  b

  c

2a

  b

  c

## 2   Understanding the language of comparison

**2a** Read these extracts from articles comparing deep and surface approaches to learning. Work in pairs. Discuss these questions.

1  What factors influence a student's approach to learning?

2  Do the following statements apply to deep learners (D), surface learners (S) or both (B)?

  **a** They value the subject they are studying.

  **b** They are focused on the requirements of the course.

  **c** They are motivated.

> Very crudely: deep learning is the best approach, better than surface learning, and teachers should teach in a way that encourages students to adopt a deep approach, although achieving this is not so easy. Perhaps the strongest influence on students' approaches to learning is assessment. It is often argued that the setting of 'straightforward' assessments involving short questions testing separate ideas will encourage surface learning. [...]

> Thus, while the engagement and actions of the learner remain central to the learning process, it is believed that better teaching creates a natural demand for deep learning in students. [...]

> Some have concluded from this that what the teacher is teaching is in fact not as important as how the students approach the subject matter. [...]

*Current educational philosophy tends to view the student as being more important than the teacher, especially with regard to independent study. Some tutors demand far more of the learner than they did in the past. [...]*

For a deep learner, the subject itself has intrinsic value. They study more dynamically than surface learners, spending extra time to fully understand the subjects that they learn. [...]

Students who take a surface approach study only what they are required to do in order to successfully complete their courses, and in this way are more passive learners than those taking a deep approach. [...]

Students taking a purely surface approach are less interested in the subjects they are studying than those taking a deep approach. [...]

Students who take a surface approach may actually be as motivated as those taking a deeper approach to their subject matter, but misunderstand what is required for success. [...]

**2b** Work in pairs. Underline any words or expressions used for comparisons in the extracts in 2a.

**Example**
... deep learning is <u>the best</u> approach, <u>better than</u> surface learning.

**2c** Complete the comparative and superlative columns in this table using some of the words and phrases you underlined in 2b.

| Adjective | Comparative | Superlative | Change |
|---|---|---|---|
| 1-syllable (e.g. *deep, strong*) | **1** *stronger* | *deepest* **2** | |
| 2-or-more syllable (e.g. *passive, important*) | **3** **4** | *most passive* *most important* | |
| 1-syllable ending consonant + vowel + consonant (e.g. *hot*) | *hott<u>er</u>* | *hott<u>est</u>* | double consonant + *-er/-est* |
| 2-syllable ending in *-y* (e.g. *happy*) | *happ<u>ier</u>* | *happ<u>iest</u>* | drop *-y* + *-ier/-iest* |
| *good* *bad* *far* | **5** *worse* *further* | **6** *worst* *furthest* | irregular |

**2d** Work in pairs. How are regular comparative and superlative adjectives formed? Write the rules in the *Change* column in the table in 2c.

**2e** Work in pairs. Choose the correct words in bold to complete these sentences. Use the information in 2c to help you.

*Example*

*Surface learners are __more reliant__ / relianter on their teachers than deep learners.*

1 Such learners tend to be **badder** / **worse** at taking responsibility for their own learning.

2 A **interestinger** / **more interesting** question is how teachers can encourage a deeper approach in classroom activities.

3 Deep learners are **more successful** / **successfuller** than surface learners at applying the knowledge they gain in their subjects to new areas.

4 Students who take a deep approach, on the other hand, are **activer** / **more active** learners.

5 It would be a mistake to characterize any student as taking a deep or surface approach all the time. Instead, it is **likelier** / **the likeliest** that students tend to adopt different approaches in different contexts.

6 The **most successful** / **more successful** students of all are likely to be those who take a blended approach.

7 There is no evidence to suggest that a deep approach means **more slow** / **slower** progress.

8 It can be challenging for teachers teaching **biger** / **bigger** classes to encourage surface learners to engage more with the subject.

---

Comparative language shows *differences* (more or less) or *equality*. You can show:

- a difference of **more** with the comparative and superlative forms in the table on p.17 (+ *than*).
- **equality** with *as … as*.
- a difference of **less** with *not as … as* or *less* (*than*) / *least*.

*Examples*

*Deep learning is […] **better than** surface learning.* (different – more)

*Students who take a surface approach may actually be **as motivated as** those taking a deeper approach.* (equal)

*Students taking a purely surface approach are **less interested** in the subjects they are studying than those taking a deep approach.* (different – less)

*What the teacher is teaching is in fact **not as important as** how the students approach the subject matter.* (different – less)

Superlative language compares somebody or something with the whole group that they/it belongs to.

*Example*

*Deep learning is **the best** approach.* (of all approaches)

*Perhaps **the strongest** influence on students' approach to learning is assessment.*

**2f** This table provides information about three educational sources. Decide if the sentences (1–5) below are true (T) or false (F). Correct the false sentences.

| | The Education Journal | Education Today magazine | www.study-blog.co.uk |
|---|---|---|---|
| Year established | 1963 | 1992 | 2004 |
| Readership 2005 | 38,000 | 184,000 | 1,100 |
| Readership today | 40,000 | 130,000 | 2,800 |
| Number of staff | 5 | 15 | 2 |
| Credibility | *** | ** | * |
| Level of analysis | *** | ** | * |
| Accuracy | *** | ** | ** |

1 *The Education Journal* is the oldest source. ____

2 *Study-blog* has a larger monthly readership than *The Education Journal*. ____

3 *The Education Journal* has a larger staff than *Education Today*. ____

4 *The Education Journal* has seen the greatest increase in readership. ____

5 *Education Today* is as credible as *The Education Journal*. ____

**2g** Write sentences comparing the educational sources using the adjectives in brackets and an appropriate comparative structure. Where only one source is given, use a superlative form. For the last two, write sentences of your own comparing the three sources.

***Example***
*The Education Journal / Study-blog (credible)*
*The Education Journal is more credible than Study-blog.*

1 *Study-blog* (analytical)

_____

2 *Education Today / The Education Journal* (credible)

_____

3 *The Education Journal* (accurate)

_____

4 the workforce at *Study-blog* / the workforce at *The Education Journal* (small)

_____

5 *Education Today / Study-blog* (accurate)

_____

6 the readership of *Education Today* in 2005 / today (small)

_____

7 *Education Today / The Education Journal* (old)

_____

8 the readership of *Study-blog* today / in 2005 (big)

_____

9

_____

10

_____

You can compare *how* something is done using comparative and superlative forms of adverbs. They are formed in a similar way to comparative and superlative adjectives. You can also use the same structures as with adjectives to show a difference of more or less and equality.

**2h** Complete the table below showing how comparative adverbs are formed using the correct form of the adverbs in this list.

| badly | dynamically | far | fast | ~~hard~~ | often | well |

| Adverb | Change | Comparative | Superlative |
| --- | --- | --- | --- |
| 1-syllable | + -er/-est | *harder*<br>1 | *the hardest*<br>2 |
| 2-or-more syllable | *more/most* + adverb | 3<br>5 | 4<br>6 |
| *well*<br>*badly*<br>*far* | irregular | 7<br>9<br>11 | 8<br>10<br>12 |

**2i** Complete the extract below from a student blog where they are reflecting on their own learning experience. Use an appropriate comparative or superlative form of the words in the list.

| concerned | few | ~~difficult~~ | easy |
| --- | --- | --- | --- |
| important | significantly | successful | deeply |

When I was at school, I didn't really know how to study and would just look over my notes the night before an exam, trying to guess the questions that would be asked. I wasn't interested in every subject I studied, which made it *more difficult* for me to motivate myself than now. Now I'm at university, studying is much _____¹ for me, as I am studying a subject that I enjoy. In the past, the _____² factor for me was getting good grades, but now I'm _____³ with learning as much about the subject as possible. My lecturers tell me that _____⁴ students read around the subject or study independently. Reading around the subject has increased my knowledge _____⁵ than just studying lecture notes and helps me support my argument when I write essays or speak in tutorials. I feel that _____⁶ students study deeply at school, but, once you enter university, you should try to study a subject _____⁷.

**3 Comparing texts and information**

**3a** Read the project assignment. What would you expect to learn on a speed reading programme and an independent study skills programme?

**Project assignment**

Examine the results of a study which compared three groups of students preparing for university study. The groups consisted of:
- students who enrolled on a **speed reading programme**
- students who enrolled on an **independent study skills programme**
- students who did neither of the above (the 'control group'*).

1 Compare the findings of the study. Work in groups.
2 Write a short report summarizing your group's findings.

\* A *control group* is used in experiments to measure experimental treatment. The results from the experimental group are compared with those of the control group, who do not receive any active treatment.

**3b** Work in pairs. Read the advertisements for the speed reading programme and the independent study skills programme examined in the study. Discuss whether you think either of the programmes is likely to help students prepare for their university studies.

**Speed reading programme**

# Attention students!

**Does it feel like there aren't enough hours in the day to study for your exams?**
**Are you tired of spending hours reading long, complex texts?**
**Do you wish there were a faster way to get the information you need?**

*'Fast Track To Speed Reading' has the solution you've been looking for.*
*In just five days, you will master the principles of Dr Robin Notso's*
*certified speed reading programme. Master the ability to:*
- *read long texts in a flash*
- *memorize key facts instantly*
- *comprehend complex ideas.*

For more information, visit www.fast-trackreading.co.uk now! What are you waiting for?
It's GUARANTEED! Get on the Fast Track today.

**Independent study skills programme**

### The approach a student takes towards learning is critical to the outcome of his/her studies.

At our university, we encourage students to get the most out of their studies at every level.

The **Independent Study Skills Programme**, led by **Dr Melvin Scott**, guides students away from shallow learning — memorization for examinations — towards a deeper understanding of their discipline. During the programme, students learn vital critical thinking skills, explore the most effective methods of independent study and learn to combine the intake of information with their own opinions to achieve a deeper level of understanding.

For more information, visit the Office of Academic Achievement.

**3c**  Read the report of the study's findings. Which programme had the highest overall success rate?

## Methods of preparation for university studies

### 1 Introduction

This report was requested by Dr Mark Hamilton, Director of the London Education Authority, on 14 August, 2011. The main aim of the report is to analyze and compare the effectiveness of a speed reading programme and an independent study skills programme as preparation for university studies.

### 2 Procedure

Data for the report was collected in November and December, 2011. Primary data was collected by testing 1,500 university students, divided into three groups of 500 students each.

**Group A:** attended the five-day speed reading programme

**Group B:** attended the five-day independent study skills programme

**Group C:** given no special training; functioned as the control group for the study

All participants were provided with identical study materials and given identical examinations at the end of the five-day period. Examinations tested students' abilities to perform on four cognitive levels: Knowledge, Comprehension, Application and Analysis (Knowledge being the least advanced cognitive level and Analysis the most). Based on exam marks, data was compiled and analyzed.

### Descriptions of cognitive levels tested

i  **Knowledge** – Requires ability to remember simple facts exactly as they were presented in study materials. Shows information has been committed to memory. Sample exercise: true/false questions

ii  **Comprehension** – Requires ability to recognize examples of the learned information. Shows basic comprehension of the material. Sample exercise: matching

iii  **Application** – Requires ability to apply information and rules to solve a problem. Shows ability to use the information or material. Sample exercise: short answer completion

iv  **Analysis** – Requires ability to deconstruct complex information and analyze how this information is related. Shows deep understanding of the material. Sample exercise: essay

### 3 Findings

Below are the median, or average, scores for each group at each level of cognitive understanding.

|  | Group A | Group B | Group C |
|---|---|---|---|
| Knowledge | 80% | 90% | 74% |
| Comprehension | 65% | 89% | 78% |
| Application | 58% | 92% | 68% |
| Analysis | 43% | 87% | 70% |

**3d**  Work in groups. Compare the findings of the study. Use comparative and superlative language in your answers. Consider these questions.

1  Which students showed a greater ability to remember simple facts?

2  Which students were more analytical?

3  How did performance change as the cognitive level became more advanced?

**3e** Write a paragraph summarizing your group's conclusions about the study. Use comparative and superlative language in your summary.

| Conclusion |
| --- |
| |

## 4 Review and extension

### Word forms

**4a** Refer back to the table of words in 1e on p.15. Write sentences for three more rows of words, illustrating the use of different word forms. Refer to your answers in 1h on p.16, but do not choose the same words.

1a

  b

  c

2a

  b

  c

3a

  b

  c

**4b** Decide whether the words in bold in these extracts from an article about approaches to learning are verbs, nouns or adjectives. Write each word in the correct column of the table below. Then complete the other columns. Use a dictionary to help you if necessary.

***Example***

*Deep learners tend to **apply** themselves to their studies: they prefer to study alone and enjoy learning new things.*

1 Deep and strategic learners **prepare** themselves well before attending lectures or participating in seminars.

2 Surface learners tend to believe that they should attend lectures only to receive **information** passively.

3 At our university, we **encourage** students to get the most out of their studies at every level.

4 During the programme, students **explore** the most effective methods of independent study.

5 Deep learning **promotes** understanding and application for life.

| Verb | Noun | Adjective |
|---|---|---|
| apply | application | applied |

**4c** Complete these sentences using the correct form of the words in brackets. Use the table in 4b to help you.

***Example***

*Many students have their <u>application</u> for funding denied. (apply)*

1 The study compared the results of students enrolled on a number of different _____ courses. (prepare)

2 Students who prepare adequately beforehand are able to get more _____ from their lectures. (inform)

3 An _____ study was conducted to investigate different learning styles. (explore)

4 Students who study in the library or common study spaces benefit from the _____ of their classmates. (encourage)

5 Well-designed academic programmes _____ independent, critical thinking. (promote)

**Using _than_ in comparisons**

**4d** Look at these examples and complete the rule below.

**_Examples_**
_Deep learning is the best approach, better_ **than** _surface learning._
_Some tutors demand far more_ **than** _they did in the past._

_Than_ normally comes immediately _____ the comparative/superlative
adjective or adverb.

> When a prepositional phrase is used, _than_ comes after the prepositional phrase,
> **not** after the comparative adjective or adverb.
>
> **_Examples_**                   comparative      prepositional phrase
> _What the learner does has become_ **more important** _for student learning_ **than**
> _what the tutor does._
>
> _Tutors are_ **more concerned** _about approaches to learning_ **than** _they used to be._
>
> _This fact has impacted_ **more significantly** _on teaching methodology_ **than** _perhaps
> any other single factor._

**4e** Read this extract from a student blog about approaches to learning at university.
The word _than_ is missing in five places in the extract. Write the word _than_ in the
correct gaps.

> While the way that students learn is of interest at all levels of education,
> it has a greater impact _____ in higher education _than_ at any other level,
> because of the focus on independent learning in university study. The way
> in which a student's approach to learning affects their success at university
> has been investigated since Marton and Säljö's pioneering study in 1976,
> which identified two different approaches to learning: deep and surface.
> Deep learners are believed to be more interested _____ in their studies _____
> surface learners. Surface learners, on the other hand, have less interest and
> tend to be less motivated to study than deep learners. Thanks to ongoing
> research in this area, our current understanding of student learning styles is
> better _____ it was _____ a few decades ago.
>
>      Though it is true that most people have a greater preference _____ for
> one approach _____ the other, studies suggest that most students are better
> _____ at switching between the two approaches _____ previously believed.
> Students tend to switch approaches based on their feelings. They are more
> likely _____ to use a deep approach _____ for subjects which they find more
> interesting _____ for subjects they dislike. On the other hand, in less popular
> subjects where the students just want to get through the course, surface
> approaches are more common than deeper ones.

# Investigating

**By the end of Part C you will be able to:**

- identify and use collocations
- use relative clauses to include essential information in sentences
- use relative clauses to include non-essential information in sentences.

## 1 Identifying and using collocations

> When you record academic vocabulary in your logbook, you should also start to record collocations used with each item.
>
> Collocations are words which commonly occur together. Some nouns usually follow particular verbs, and are not usually used with other verbs. Compare these sentences:
>
> *Dr McNeil gives very interesting lectures.*
>
> NOT *Dr McNeil performs very interesting lectures.*
>
> Most native speakers would say that the first sentence sounds more correct than the second. This is because the word *lecture* is commonly used with the verb *give*, but is not normally used with the verb *perform*. In other words, *give a lecture* is a collocation. An understanding of collocations will not only help your writing to appear more natural, but will also make listening to lectures easier.

**1a** Read this text about different types of research and write notes about the major differences between primary and secondary research. Discuss your understanding of the differences with a partner.

At some point in your studies you will be expected to do further **research** yourself. This could be for the purpose of building your knowledge, or perhaps to write an essay or report, or it may be that you have to do an original piece of **research** for a longer project or thesis. Generally speaking, you are likely to have some **involvement** in the following three types of research.

*Tutor-guided* **research**
The student is introduced to a topic and encouraged to learn more by their tutor, who may provide a reading list of both key and supplementary **texts** for the student to investigate.

*Student-led secondary* **research**
Students do some kind of **research** project on their own, searching for **texts** and information by themselves. The students do not gather **data** directly, but use **data** published by other researchers. They need to use the **resources** of a library to collect **data** on a large scale and reach **conclusions**. It also allows students to find out gaps in knowledge which may form the basis for new enquiry. The students have the **responsibility** for finding new information by themselves.

*Student-led primary* **research**
When a topic has not been studied before, the student/researcher conducts an **investigation** to produce original results through fieldwork, direct observation or experiment. The student/researcher is responsible for finding new **data** independently.

**1b** Look at the nouns in bold in the text in 1a and the words around them. Identify which words are used with the nouns in bold, and write the collocations in the second column of the table.

| Noun in text | Collocations from the text | Other collocations |
|---|---|---|
| *research* | | |
| *involvement* | | |
| *texts* | | |
| *data* | *gather data, use data, collect data, finding data* | *analyze data, data-bank, data processing, data protection* |
| *resources* | | |
| *conclusions* | | |
| *responsibility* | | |
| *investigation* | | |

**1c** Work in pairs. Think of other words that are commonly used with the nouns in bold. Write them in the third column of the table. Use a dictionary to help you.

**1d** Work in groups. Write five sentences about university study using collocations from the table in 1b.

**1e** Compare your sentences with another group.

## 2 Using relative clauses to include essential information in sentences

**2a** Work in pairs. Read the extract below from a university study guide and discuss these questions.

1 What types of sources are students expected to use?

2 What types of books and articles are usually included in a reading list?

> Tutors may provide a reading list containing recommended sources. Students are expected to use the sources which are on the reading list to help them complete assignments. However, students are also encouraged to use sources which are not on the reading list as well. The reading list normally recommends books and articles that are available through the university library.

> The underlined relative clauses in the sentences below provide information to help identify the nouns in bold. They give information which tells you which noun is being spoken about.
>
> *Students are expected to use the* **sources** *which are on the reading list to help them complete assignments.*
>
> *However, students are also encouraged to use* **sources** *which are not on the reading list as well.*
>
> *The reading list normally recommends* **books and articles** *that are available through the university library.*

**2b** Work in pairs. If the relative clauses are removed from the sentences above, is the information about the nouns complete?

> The relative clauses above are called *defining relative clauses*: they give information which is essential to your understanding of the noun and cannot be removed from a sentence without affecting your ability to identify the noun.
>
> *Students are expected to use the* **sources**. (we don't know which sources)
>
> *Students are expected to use the* **sources** *which are on the reading list to help them complete assignments.* (this tells us which sources)

**2c** Complete the table below using the words and phrases in this list.

~~people/organizations~~     people/things     places     possession     time

| Relative pronoun | Use | Example |
|---|---|---|
| who | refers to people/ organizations | *He found that the* **students** *who read the script actually got more benefit from it than* **those** *who did not.* |
| which/that | refers to 1 _____ | *Teachers need to construct* **assessment** *that gives students the opportunity to receive feedback.* |
| whose | shows 2 _____ | **Lecturers** *whose notes are available online may be significantly aiding their students' understanding.* |
| where | refers to 3 _____ | *Most university campuses have* **a place** *where students can go to get advice and support with their studies.* |
| when | refers to 4 _____ | *Tutorials are* **the time** *when tutors can assess how much progress their students are making.* |

**2d** Underline the relative pronouns used in the sentences (a–g). Then decide which could be replaced with *that*.

**a** Find a study skills guide <u>which</u> gives more advice about improving your research skills.

**b** These allow students to search for the material which they want in various ways.

**c** You need to make sure to keep the students with whom you work informed of your progress.

**d** Students generally work harder for lecturers who they like.

**e** Students who are organized have an easier time completing assignments on time.

**f** If you are lucky, you should find a lot of sources which could be useful.

**g** There are many different ways in which this information can be written.

---

*Which* and *that* can be used interchangeably as the object of defining relative clauses.

**Example**

*These allow students to search for the material **which/that** they want in various ways.*

*Whom* is used after prepositions. It is more common in writing than speech. In very formal contexts, *whom* can be used as the object of a relative clause.

**Example**

*Prizes will be awarded to students **whom** the university considers to have performed exceptionally during their course.*

---

**2e** Complete these sentences using an appropriate relative pronoun. There may be more than one possible answer.

**Example**

*The tutor has specialist knowledge <u>which</u> they pass on to their students in lectures and tutorials.*

**1** Mastering a new subject is an experience _____ is often frustrating.

**2** If you are struggling with an assignment, it is important to try and find someone _____ can help you, such as a classmate.

**3** There are many different ways in _____ coursework can be approached.

**4** There is usually a point _____ students can ask questions at the end of every lecture.

**5** The student union is the place _____ many students meet to socialize after class.

**2f** Work in pairs. Finish these sentences by adding a defining relative clause.

**1** Students go to <u>lectures</u>

_____

**2** The library has many <u>books</u>

_____

**3** Choose a good <u>research partner</u>

_____

**4** There are a number of <u>journal articles</u>

_____

**5** There is a <u>resource area</u> in the library

_____

**6** A tutor is a <u>person</u>

_____

## 3 Using relative clauses to include non-essential information in sentences

**3a** Read the extract below from a study guide entry about journals and answer these questions.

1 What can you find in a journal?

2 What is in a volume of a journal?

A journal, which is a kind of academic magazine, contains articles about the latest research in a particular academic field and comments and reviews of existing research. Scholars involved in the field, who often conduct research as part of a larger team, are invited to submit articles to the journal, detailing their research. A single issue of a journal is like a single issue of a magazine; it contains several articles, as well as book reviews, comments and other news. These issues are collected into volumes, where all the issues for a particular period are bound together into something like a large book. For example, in 2001, the Harvard Law Review published its 114th volume, containing the collected eight issues of that journal published during the previous year.

> The underlined relative clauses in these sentences provide additional information about the nouns in bold.
>
> *A **journal**, <u>which is a kind of academic magazine</u>, contains articles about the latest research in a particular academic field and comments and reviews of existing research.*
>
> *These issues are collected into **volumes**, <u>where all issues for a particular period are bound together into a large book</u>.*
>
> The relative clauses above are called *non-defining relative clauses*. They give extra, or non-essential, information about a noun. If a non-defining relative clause is removed from a sentence, it does not affect the meaning of the noun.
>
> Commas are used to separate the relative clause from the main clause.
>
> *That* cannot be used in a non-defining relative clause.

**3b** Work in pairs. Discuss whether each of these statements is true (T) or false (F).

1 If a non-defining relative clause is removed, the sentence is still grammatically correct and makes sense. _____

2 Non-defining relative clauses need commas. _____

3 The relative pronoun *who* can be used in defining relative clauses but not non-defining relative clauses. _____

4 Non-defining relative clauses provide important or essential information about the noun. _____

5 The relative pronoun *that* can be used in a non-defining relative clause. _____

**3c** Underline the relative clauses in these extracts from a student study guide.

*Example*

*Internet sources, <u>which students find extremely convenient</u>, sometimes contain information of questionable value.*

1 Online search engines, which are becoming increasingly indispensable as resources, are sometimes not allowed as sources for academic work.

**2** The student is introduced to a topic by their tutor, who will provide a reading list of relevant resources.

**3** Renowned scholars, who are invited by journals to submit articles, appreciate the recognition that they receive when their research is published.

**4** Many other students, with whom you will be sharing these resources, will need to borrow the same journals, so plan your research time accordingly.

**3d** Work in pairs. Discuss these questions.

**1** What is the subject of each relative clause in 3c?

**2** What is the difference between *who* and *whom*?

**3e** Complete the sentences below with the relative pronouns in this list.

when  where  which  which  ~~who~~  whom

*Example*
*A research librarian, <u>who</u> helps students with research projects, is available daily.*

**1** Some students try to study every night, _____ means they don't have to cram before exams.

**2** All students are issued with a library card, _____ gives them access to the library's extensive collection of books and journals.

**3** Students will be allocated to lecturers, to _____ they should submit their assignments.

**4** The Students' Union, _____ many students choose to study, is open late every night.

**5** During the vacations, _____ many students go home or travel, the library has reduced opening hours.

**3f** Choose a clause from each column of the table to make sentences containing non-defining relative clauses.

| Column 1 | Column 2 | Column 3 |
|---|---|---|
| **1** The student is introduced to a topic | **a** who can be contacted via email, | **i** which lists synonyms and antonyms of words. |
| **2** Besides a dictionary, | **b** enjoy visiting the city at the weekend, | **ii** who may provide a reading list of both key and supplementary texts for the student to investigate. |
| **3** For each subject, | **c** you might find it useful to use a thesaurus, | **iii** may agree to extend the deadline of a term paper. |
| **4** Lecturers, | **d** where students can get study advice, | **iv** which will give details of the relevant published articles and text books. |
| **5** There is a student services office on campus, | **e** and encouraged to learn more by the tutor, | **v** when they don't have classes. |
| **6** University students | **f** you will be supplied with a full reading list, | **vi** as well as information about accommodation, sports and social events. |

**3g** Choose four items from this list and write a complete sentence about each.

- homework assignments
- the college library
- many lecturers
- the use of electronic translators
- distance learning
- the study of English language
- China
- the students in my class
- William Shakespeare
- the best approach to learning vocabulary

*Example*
*China is one of the world's largest economies.*

**3h** Work in pairs. Exchange sentences. Add extra information to each of your partner's sentences using a non-defining relative clause.

*Example*
*China, which hosted the 2008 Olympics, is one of the world's largest economies.*

> **LESSON TASK**    **4 Describing features of academic work**

**4a** Read the text below on 'Writing a research paper'. Write brief notes in the table on p.34 about the key features of the words in bold.

## Writing a research paper

Writing a **research paper** is a daunting task, and one which many students must complete. A research paper is a long essay. It is usually written by students at the end of their semester or academic year. For most students, it takes a couple of months, but for others it can take much longer. For the first step of the research paper process, the student must come up with a new and interesting topic. A certain amount of reading and research is needed before selecting the exact topic. When enough information is collected on the subject, a student is able to write a **thesis statement** and a **research proposal**. The thesis statement explains the purpose of the essay, often involving a problem or a question. It is the main idea and is often an opinion or an argument. A research proposal is a summary of what the student will cover in the research paper. The research proposal is usually between 5 and 15 pages long and provides general information about where the student will get his or her information. Next, the student's **advisor** must approve the topic. An advisor is a lecturer who works closely with the student and reads the student's research proposal and assesses the topic for research. If the advisor believes that it is a good subject, he or she will allow the student to continue the research.

The best place to start researching is the university library. Every library has a **library catalogue**, which is usually online, and contains a list of all of the resources in the library. Using the library catalogue, students can search by author, title, or subject. Here, students can find both **primary sources** and **secondary sources** for their research. Primary sources are original materials and have not been interpreted or changed. Examples of primary sources include letters and emails, diaries, newspaper articles (written at the time in question), research surveys, original documents and government/organization records. Secondary sources are written after the time in question and are often interpreted by a second party. **Encyclopaedias** are an example of a secondary source. They contain articles, listed in alphabetical order, on many topics and branches of knowledge. Other examples include textbooks, biographies, critical works, articles, dictionaries and magazines.

After the research has been completed, it is time for the student to start writing the research paper. A typical research paper can be as long as 100 pages, so it is very important to be organized. It is often helpful to begin with an **outline**. An outline is a plan which details the order in which information will be presented, keeping the writer organized and the writing well-structured. At this time, it is also important to put together a **list of references** or a bibliography. Both of these provide details of the sources of information, including author, title of text, date and city of publication, publisher, page number or website. It is very important that credit is given to all of the sources used to avoid plagiarizing someone's work. **Plagiarism** is when a person uses someone else's ideas or words as their own. This can be the result of deliberate cheating – a student copying work which they know is not their own – or can happen by accident, if the student is not skilled at using references. Plagiarism is often referred to as a kind of 'academic theft', and it can be punished severely. It is crucial to avoid plagiarizing – even if done by accident. Once the writing is complete, the last step is to revise and proofread the work. **Proofreading** involves looking for mistakes which were made during the writing process. They can involve spelling, grammar, punctuation, and factual mistakes. Once these are corrected, the research paper is ready to be submitted.

| Writing a research paper | |
| --- | --- |
| research paper | • Long essay<br>• Written at the end of a semester or academic year<br>• Can take months to complete |
| thesis statement | |
| research proposal | |
| advisor | |

| | |
|---|---|
| library catalogue | |
| primary source | |
| secondary source | |
| encyclopaedia | |
| outline | |
| list of references | |
| plagiarism | |
| proofreading | |

**4b** Check your notes in pairs.

**4c** Work in pairs. Write five sentences about writing a research paper. Each sentence should include one of the words from the table in 4a and a relative clause based on the information in the table.

*Example*
*Students generally submit research papers, which can take months to complete, at the end of a semester or academic year.*

<table>
<tr><td>1</td><td></td></tr>
<tr><td>2</td><td></td></tr>
<tr><td>3</td><td></td></tr>
<tr><td>4</td><td></td></tr>
<tr><td>5</td><td></td></tr>
</table>

## 5 Review and extension

**Writing non-defining relative clauses**

**5a** Complete each of these sentences with a non-defining relative clause.

*Example*

*Subjects like Economics and Business, <u>which are increasingly popular,</u> have a lot of required reading.*

1 Students living in halls of residence, _____, will be in contact with people from many different backgrounds.

2 The popularity of the course is due to the reputation of the lecturer, _____.

3 Studying Art and Design in the heart of London, _____, has some obvious advantages.

4 Research projects, _____, are often completed over a period of several months.

5 Deadlines, _____, can only be changed in special circumstances.

6 'Short loan' books, which are very popular, can only be borrowed for three days. However, 'regular loan books', _____, can be borrowed for up to a week.

7 Journal articles, _____, can be found online or in the library.

8 The bibliography, _____, is due tomorrow.

9 Primary research, _____, has advantages and disadvantages.

## Using *whose* in relative clauses

Look at the sentences below. Notice how the sentences are combined using the relative pronoun *whose*.

*Ference Marton and Roger Säljö first introduced the idea of deep and surface approaches in a pioneering 1976 study. They claimed that students might employ either method depending on the circumstances.*

*Ference Marton and Roger Säljö,* **whose** *pioneering 1976 study first introduced the idea of deep and surface approaches, claimed that students might employ either method depending on the circumstances.*

In the example, *whose* is used to show the study belongs to Säljö and Marton. *Whose* is used to show ownership and can be used for people or objects.

**5b** Combine these pairs of sentences into single sentences using the relative pronoun *whose*.

1 The students' work is turned in after the deadline. Their work will not be given a mark.

2 The library's collection of resources is the most comprehensive. Those libraries will be the most useful for your research.

3 Donaldson is a researcher. His work has been widely published.

## Using quantifiers in relative clauses

You can use non-defining relative clauses to talk about a quantity or part of something.

**5c** Work in pairs. Read the sentences (a–c) below and answer these questions.

1 How many of the recommended resources are available at the library?

2 How many of the search engine results were helpful?

3 How many students are doing the same topic?

a The lecturer has provided a list of recommended resources, all of which are available at the library.

b The search engine returned an abundant number of results, none of which were helpful.

c There are ten students, all of whom are doing the same topic, using the same resources.

A quantifier + *of* + *whom/which* can be used with a non-defining relative clause to specify a particular quantity or amount. You use *whom* for people and *which* for things.

Here are some quantifiers commonly used in this way.

**With countable nouns:** all; few; many; most; none; one, two, three, etc.; some; two per cent; etc.

**With uncountable nouns:** all; most; much; none; some; two per cent; etc.

**5d** Complete these sentences by underlining the correct words in bold.

*Example*

*This term you will take three modules, all of <u>which</u> / whom will require writing a research paper.*

1 There are three other international students in your residence, two of **which / whom** are from Asia.

2 In class, you will get a lot of input, **many / much** of which you will need to remember.

3 That class has four required research papers, **all of which / all which** are due after the Christmas holiday.

4 There are three types of research, two of **which / whom** are student-led.

5 I found a range of sources, **none / none of which** were on the reading list.

6 There are many different ways to reference your sources, **two / one** of which is the Harvard style.

7 This journal contains relevant material, **most / many** of which you can use for your research.

8 The university has two libraries, one of **whom / which** is devoted to business material.

9 There are many well-known professors here, most of **whom / which** have had books published.

# Reporting in speech

**By the end of Part D you will be able to:**

- recognize and use the language of academic discussions
- refer to other people's ideas in discussion.

## 1 Recognizing and using the language of academic discussions

> There are many differences between informal conversations and the formal discussions you are likely to be involved in during a tutorial class, an individual tutorial or study group.

**1a** Work in groups. Discuss the differences between informal conversations and academic discussions. Give specific examples to back up your ideas. Write notes in the table below.

| Informal conversations | Academic discussions |
|---|---|
|  |  |

**1b** Compare your ideas with the rest of the class.

**1c** Work in pairs. Make a list of what you can do before, during and after a tutorial class to get the most out of it.

| Before | During | After |
|---|---|---|
|  |  |  |

1.7

**1d** Listen to a group of students talking about making the most of a tutorial discussion. Write notes of suggestions they make about what you should do *before* and *during* a tutorial class.

**1e** Work in pairs. Read the transcript of the discussion you have just listened to and answer these questions. Underline the relevant sections in the transcript.

**1** How does Susan get the discussion started?

**2** How does Mohammed indicate that he doesn't know what to do?

**3** How does Martha agree with what Susan has said?

**4** How does David change the direction of the conversation? What does he do before he suggests a change in direction?

**5** Martha and David disagree with each other. What do they both do to make their disagreement less 'direct' or less confrontational?

**6** How does Susan bring Mohammed into the discussion?

**7** What expression does Mohammed use to suggest a solution to the disagreement?

| | |
|---|---|
| **Susan:** | So, we've been asked to discuss what people need to do during a tutorial. What kinds of things are likely to lead to a successful discussion? |
| **Mohammed:** | Sorry, Susan, I'm not sure I understand exactly. What do you mean by 'What people need to do'? Do you mean, like, we should read up on the topic before the tutorial? |
| **Susan:** | Yes, exactly. Or, for example, we should make a note of any questions we have on the reading. |
| **Martha:** | Absolutely! I also think it's important to record where we found the readings so we can reference them properly. We should keep accurate records of all … |
| **David:** | I'm sorry to interrupt, Martha – you're absolutely right, but I think we're supposed to focus on what we should be doing during the discussion, rather than how we should prepare for it. I think we should be looking at things like how we help other people to contribute during the discussion, or how we should take turns to speak – not talking over the top of others, things like that, you know? |
| **Martha:** | Well, I can see that those sorts of things are important in a discussion, but I'm not sure I agree that that's the only thing we should be talking about. I think how you prepare for a discussion is really important in deciding what you do during the discussion. |
| **David:** | I totally agree, Martha. How you prepare is, of course, vitally important. I'm just saying that I think in this discussion now, we should focus on what to do during the tutorial itself. What do the rest of you think? |
| **Susan:** | Yes, I think David might be right. I do remember the tutor mentioning things like 'turn-taking' and 'checking understanding'. Mohammed, help us out here. What do you think? |
| **Mohammed:** | Well, perhaps we could do both if we're not sure – just to make sure we cover everything? |
| **David:** | You're right, Mohammed. Let's do that. Yes, let's cover *before*, *during* and even *after* the tutorial – we're bound to be well prepared that way! Sorry, Martha, what were you saying about keeping records? |

**1f** Write the expressions you underlined in the transcript on p.39 in the correct row in the table below.

| Function | Examples of expressions |
|---|---|
| Getting a discussion started | |
| Checking understanding or asking for clarification | |
| Indicating agreement | |
| Changing the topic of the discussion | |
| Disagreeing politely with another speaker | |
| Helping others contribute to the discussion | |
| Making recommendations or suggestions | |

**1g** Work in pairs. Think of more expressions and add them to each row.

**1h** You are going to have a discussion about approaches to learning. Read these questions and write notes of your ideas in the table below.

1 What is the best way to help students understand the importance of taking a *deep approach** to learning?

2 What kinds of learning activities are best for encouraging a deep approach to learning?

3 What kind of approach to learning is encouraged in the education system in your own country?

4 What are the benefits of a *surface approach*** to learning?

\* With a deep approach to learning, students are interested in the subject matter and want to understand and engage with it fully.

\*\* With a surface approach, students only want to understand as much as is necessary in order to get good grades rather than develop a full knowledge of the topic.

| Notes |
|---|
|  |

**1i** Work in small groups. Discuss the questions in 1h. Try to use some of the expressions in 1f during your discussion.

## 2 Referring to other people's ideas in discussion

**2a** Work in pairs. Discuss these questions and write your ideas below.

1 What do you understand by a *gap year*? Who has a gap year? What kinds of things do people do on a gap year?

2 What are the advantages and disadvantages of taking a gap year?

3 Would you take (or have you taken) a gap year? Give details.

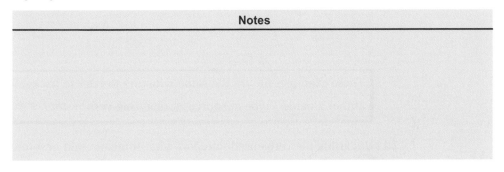

| What a gap year is |
|---|
|  |

| Advantages | Disadvantages |
|---|---|
|  |  |

**2b** Listen to three students discussing the question 'Is taking a gap year beneficial for students?' Were your ideas in 2a mentioned by the students? Add to your notes if necessary.

1.8

**2c** In the discussion, each of the students tried to support their ideas by referring to something they had read on the subject. Listen again and complete.

| Ben | Kim | Sarah |
|---|---|---|
| Nick Smith _____ in his most recent book that … | An article I was reading _____ that … | … an article I read _____ that … |

> These examples all use the same structure to refer to background reading:
>
> author's name / type of source + reporting verb + *that* + statement

**2d** Underline the verbs used to report what someone said or wrote in these sentences.

*Example*
*Isaacs <u>found</u> that academic staff tend to share a common understanding of the purposes of lectures.*

1 MacManaway established that students who read transcripts of lectures get more benefit than those who simply listen to their lectures.

2 The newspaper claims that the number of people using Facebook is increasing rapidly in East and Central Africa.

3 Symon Wanda argues that launching a Swahili version of Facebook will help to preserve the language.

4 Houghton states that teachers need to make assessments relevant to the real world.

5 Lukow observed that little research has been done to investigate the relationship between classroom IT and student learning styles.

6 Cox points out that continued advances in IT bring increasing challenges for educational institutions.

> You can use reporting verbs to report something that the writer or speaker has established through research, or to report an opinion. Compare these sentences:
>
> 1 *Jones **proved** that students who take gap years get better grades on average.*
> 2 *Jones **argues** that students who take gap years get better grades on average.*
>
> The first sentence suggests that Jones has done research which shows a clear link between gap years and student success – it can be accepted as a fact and it is unlikely that people would disagree with it. However, in the second sentence, Jones is only giving his opinion; other people may disagree.

**2e** Work in pairs. Write the reporting verbs in this list in the correct column of the table below.

argue    ~~claim~~    demonstrate    establish    find    observe

point out    prove    show    state    suggest

| Reporting things established through research | Reporting opinions |
| --- | --- |
|  | *claim* |

**2f** Are the sentences in 2d reporting the results of research or opinions?

**2g** Work in groups. Brainstorm other reporting verbs. Discuss whether each verb reports the results of research or opinions. Write the verbs in the correct column of the table in 2e.

**2h** Read this extract from a newspaper article. Why do some educators think that taking a gap year could be good for students?

> The Prime Minister has stated his plans to back gap years by providing scholarships to fund millions of sixth-form graduates and university-leavers. The gap year is a year taken off from studies either before or after university, when young people can spend time volunteering, working, travelling, or completing an apprenticeship. The opposition has said the proposed bill 'is wasteful, useless, and has zero chance of being passed'. However, some educators are welcoming the proposal. They suggest that if students have five days of school each week from the age of six, it's easy for them to become burned out. Some time off might be the perfect way to make students more focused and responsible the next time they return to the laboratory or the library.

**2i** Complete these sentences reporting information from the article in 2h using appropriate reporting verbs.

**1** The article _____ that gap years may help students to focus when they eventually enter university.

**2** The article _____ that the proposed scholarships have little chance of going ahead.

**3** An article I read _____ that the Prime Minister supports gap years.

# 3 Conducting an effective discussion

**3a** You are going to take part in a small group discussion on the question 'Is taking a gap year beneficial for students?'

Read the four extracts below and underline any **information** or **language** which you think may be useful to you during the discussion.

Most of what is written nowadays will argue in favour of gap years, but one has to consider who is writing. If there is a connection to a tour company, for example, then the content of what is written may be compromised. There are many disadvantages facing gap year students that may be overlooked. The biggest disadvantage is that whilst a student is on their gap year they are probably not thinking about their studies, and when they enter university will be considerably behind other students who have just left school.

Hartog, S. (2010, June 6th). Why are gap years so popular? *The Glasgow Star*, p.15.

Why take a gap year? Students who spent their gap year travelling abroad with Sandstorm Travel stress that it gave them some much needed time to relax and consider their future. They may have travelled abroad hoping to study one subject on their return, but whilst they were away had an experience that changed their hopes for the future. It's much better to experience that desire to change before you embark upon a university course and to change your course at university before it is too late. Choosing the right course makes students less likely to drop out of university. A gap year gives students the time to reflect that they wouldn't get if they just entered university straight after high school.

Sandstorm Travel (2009). *Sandstorm Travel Brochure*. Retrieved July 1st 2010 from http://www.sandstormtravel.com/

The results of our survey indicate that of the problems associated with gap years, the risk of injury is the biggest concern for parents, whereas students are most concerned that the year will be a disappointment. Some gap years might cost students or their parents more money than they will save, and, although it could be sold as 'an experience of a lifetime', it runs the risk of appearing like a long holiday to employers. This is another worry to the students interviewed. The results suggest that students should research gap years carefully and consider exactly what they want to gain from it before committing themselves to any gap year project.

Denton, M. & Edwards, K. (2009). An investigation into pre-gap year fears. *Education Monthly*, *13*(2), 30–46.

If students plan a gap year abroad that gives them work experience, and perhaps even paid work, it could be of tremendous advantage to their life at university and beyond. If, for example, a student wishes to study a language at university, living in a country where that language is spoken for up to a year will improve their fluency and be of tremendous benefit to their studies. If a student gains employment for that year, they could save money that would help pay for their tuition fees or living costs. Finally, if they gain work experience that is related to their future career, they will have a huge advantage over other graduates, who often know a lot about a particular subject, but have no practical experience.

Wright, J. (2010). *What to do next? A guide for students*. London: Brampton House

**3b** Work in groups of four. Discuss the question 'Is taking a gap year beneficial for students?' Try to come to an agreement before you finish speaking. Use the expressions in 1f.

## 4 Review and extension

### Reporting verbs

**4a** Choose the most suitable words in bold to complete these sentences.

*Example*
*Birch and Miller (2007) compared the results of Australian students who progressed straight to university with those who took gap years. They* **demonstrated** */* **said** *that students who took gap years tended to get higher grades at university.*

1 Birch and Miller (2007) **believe / observed** that this trend is particularly clear among male students.

2 Hartog (2010) **argues / proves** that a gap year may be disadvantageous to students.

3 O'Reilly's (2006) study **established / claimed** that backpacking was associated with dropping out and failure.

4 Wright (2010) **suggests / proves** that students gain positive experiences from a gap year.

5 A study by Jones (2005) **has found / has said** that volunteer activities are becoming increasingly popular.

### The language of discussions

1.9

**4b** Listen to two people talking about their gap years and write notes in the table below for the questions (1–6).

| | Katie Davies | Emily Walker |
|---|---|---|
| 1 Where did they go? | | |
| 2 What did they do? | | |
| 3 What problems did they face? | | |
| 4 Did they overcome their problems? How? | | |
| 5 How did they benefit from the gap year? | | |
| 6 What effects did the gap year have on them once they returned home? | | |

**4c** Prepare a short talk on the question: 'Is taking a gap year beneficial for students?'
- Refer to the experiences of the two gap-year students in 4b.
- Make use of any information from this Part and your own experience or the experience of people you know, to justify your main points.
- Outline the main advantages and disadvantages of taking a gap year.

# Reporting in writing

**By the end of Part E you will be able to:**
- understand general features of academic writing
- use compound nouns
- write in a formal register.

## 1   Understanding general features of academic writing

Although there are different styles within academic writing, most academic writing demonstrates similar features. The language is **objective**, **impersonal** and **precise**:

- using formal alternatives (e.g. *little* and *a great deal* rather than *not much* and *lots of*)
- avoiding personal pronouns such as *you* and *I*
- avoiding the use of direct questions
- avoiding contractions (e.g. *won't, didn't, we'll*, etc.)
- acknowledging sources of information with clear and accurate references.

**1a**   Read the beginning of an essay on English language learning styles and underline any features which do not follow the guidelines above.

### English language learning styles (1)

We all know that students have their own individual styles of learning. Learning styles are a hot topic for analysis nowadays. One expert says that there are six different general learning styles. Do you know what they are called? They are dependent, independent, collaborative, competitive, participant and avoidant. However, for learning English specifically, another expert says there are only four different styles. They are the concrete, the analytical, the communicative and the authority-oriented. In the following paragraphs, I'll tell you about this four-way classification. Then I'll explain some of the pros and cons of each one.

**1b**   Check your answers with a partner.

**1c** Work in pairs. Read the same section of the essay in 1a rewritten in a more appropriate academic style. Discuss how the examples of less appropriate language use in the first extract have been improved in the second extract. Identify any features in the second version which do not appear at all in the first.

## English language learning styles (2)

The significant increase in research into learning styles over the last decade indicates that individual students learn in different ways. In the field of general education, Claxton & Murrell (1987, p.20) have identified six basic types of learning styles and these are presented as three sets of contrasting pairs: dependent/independent, collaborative/competitive, participant/avoidant. Nunan (1991, p.16), however, refined these general learning styles by proposing styles specifically related to English language learning: the concrete, the analytical, the communicative and the authority-oriented.

This paper will first discuss a classification of learning styles from the field of general education and then go on to examine different individual styles in learning English specifically, considering the positive and negative characteristics of each style.

### References

Claxton, C. & Murrell, D. (1987). *Learning styles*. California: Sage

Nunan, D. (1991). *Language learning*. London: Longman

## 2 Stating aims in a formal register

Traditionally, the use of the pronoun *I* has been discouraged in academic writing. However, its use varies between different academic disciplines, and some academic writers feel that its use is acceptable when stating your aims in a presentation or written paper. Generally, though, its use should be kept to a minimum. You should check with your tutors to find out what they prefer.

**2a** Read this draft introduction to a student essay. Identify ways in which it might be improved.

I'm going to write this essay about whether students who're taking a distance learning degree should have to take a language course or not. Distance learning is a hot topic these days. There are lots of arguments on both sides of this discussion, so it's not easy to take a position. I, however, think that if you're taking a distance learning degree you shouldn't have to take a language course.

**2b** Read this email from the student's tutor and check your answers to 2a. Rewrite the introduction in a more appropriate style.

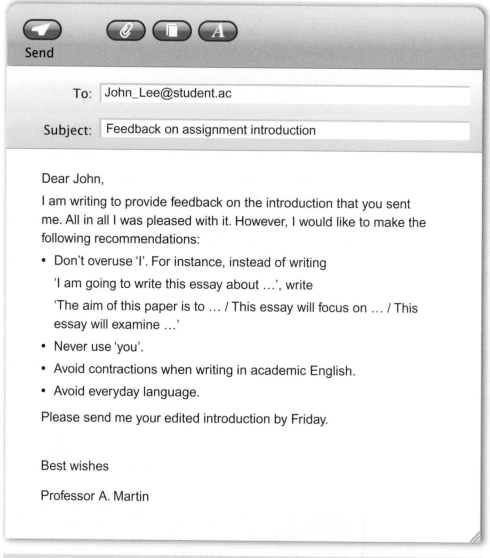

Send

To: John_Lee@student.ac

Subject: Feedback on assignment introduction

Dear John,

I am writing to provide feedback on the introduction that you sent me. All in all I was pleased with it. However, I would like to make the following recommendations:

• Don't overuse 'I'. For instance, instead of writing

  'I am going to write this essay about …', write

  'The aim of this paper is to … / This essay will focus on … / This essay will examine …'

• Never use 'you'.

• Avoid contractions when writing in academic English.

• Avoid everyday language.

Please send me your edited introduction by Friday.


Best wishes

Professor A. Martin

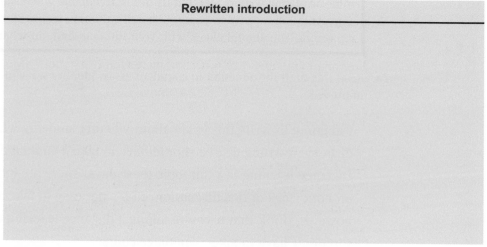

**Rewritten introduction**

**2c** Compare your answers with a partner. Explain the reasons for the changes you made.

**2d**  Work in pairs. Read this introduction to an essay on the benefits of working while studying. Rewrite the introduction in an appropriate academic style.

## Working while studying

I'm going to write about whether it's better to have a job whilst studying at university or not. I think it's better to have a job whilst studying. This is because it gives you a better experience of life and students can borrow less money. I'll explain how many students stay on campus, study on campus and chat only with other students and university workers. Some people say that this is good for students. It makes them think only about their studies. I think that students need to experience life on the streets as well. This gives them a bigger education. Another point I'll write about is as well as getting a great education, students will be better off working whilst studying. They'll finish university owing less. Attending university today can cost a lot of money. Students often leave university thousands of pounds in the red. If students work part-time whilst studying, they will bring down the amount of debt. Lastly, I think that working whilst studying at university is a good thing. We get work experience and shrink our student debt.

**2e**  Work in groups of four. Read what the other pair has written and make suggestions for how it could be improved.

## 3  Using compound nouns

Compound nouns are a very common feature of academic language. A compound noun is a combination of two or more nouns.

*Example*
*Teaching methodologies vary widely from country to country.*

The order of the nouns is important to the meaning. The first noun acts like an adjective, describing the second noun.

*Example*
*teaching methodologies* (what type of methodology? Teaching)

A compound noun can consist of more than two words.

*Example*
*University teaching methodologies*

**3a**  Work in pairs. Discuss the differences in meaning between these pairs of compound nouns.

1 technology integration      integration technology
2 library catalogue      catalogue library
3 designer software      software designer

**3b** Read this text about the use of technology in the classroom and its relationship to students' learning styles. Why, according to the text, will an increase in the use of technology in the classroom mean that individual learning styles will need to be considered much more carefully?

> There are several issues that may arise when technology is applied in the classroom. Among these are (a) choices about which technology to use (Banks et al., 2002), (b) how effective technologies are in reinforcing learning (Gerrard, 1996) and (c) technology's role in shifting the focus away from tutors and towards students (Institute of Learning, n.d.). Shifting the classroom perspective from tutors to students must involve recognizing the learning styles of students. Subsequently, tutors must adjust teaching strategies to accommodate different styles. Given the amount of literature about how 'learning style' is actually defined, the following definition addresses the role of the individual in learning.
>
> Learning style can be defined as the general tendency towards a particular learning approach displayed by an individual (Keith & Farrell, 1990; Rocha, 1999). In other words, students may prefer one approach to learning over other approaches. If the goal of educators is to increase learning outcomes, addressing the issues involved in using technology in the classroom and accommodating student learning styles must be examined. Although there are studies addressing the issues of technology integration into the curriculum and the attitudes of students towards the technology being used, there is limited research that links student attitudes to individual learning styles (Lucas, 2002).

**3c** Check your answers with a partner.

**3d** Read the text again and underline all the compound nouns. Are there any compound nouns with more than two words?

**Restating compound nouns as prepositional phrases**

> A compound noun can be rephrased using prepositions to join the nouns instead.
>
> *Examples*
>
> | **Compound noun** | **Noun + preposition + noun** |
> |---|---|
> | *climate change* | *change in climate* |
> | *student feedback* | *feedback from students* |
> | *technology integration* | *integration of technology* |
> | *integration technology* | *technology of integration* |

**3e** Work in pairs. Write the compound nouns from the text in 3b in the table below. Then rephrase them using a preposition.

| Compound noun | Noun + preposition + noun |
| --- | --- |
| | |
| | |
| | |
| | |

**3f** Underline more examples of prepositional noun phrases in the text in 3b.

> **LESSON TASK**  **4 Writing in a formal register**

1.10

**4a** Listen to an extract from a lecture on distance learning. Write notes as you listen and then answer these questions.

**1** Was the lecture formal or informal? How do you know?

**2** What do you think the previous lecture was about?

**4b** Use the essay notes below to write a short essay on this title: *Outline the advantages and disadvantages of distance learning*. The introduction has been written for you.

**Introduction**
The aim of this paper is to evaluate the advantages and disadvantages of distance learning. Distance learning has fast become a popular alternative to attending university in person and most institutions now offer a number of courses online. It is, however, still inconclusive as to whether students who are taking these courses are as well served as those who still attend in person. This paper will look at issues around technology, work rate, and student–teacher contact to argue that the positives of distance learning far outweigh the negatives.

**Body paragraph 1 – technology**

Advantages – learn computer skills, engaging, flexible location

Disadvantages – expensive, technical complications

**Body paragraph 2 – work rate**

Advantages – fit into own schedule, choose the most productive time/place for you, flexible

Disadvantages – must be self-disciplined

**Body paragraph 3 – student–teacher contact**

Advantages – can email any time, small webinars, still have face-to-face contact through web

Disadvantages – face-to-face communication development

**Conclusion**

## 5 Review and extension

### Using an academic style of writing

**5a** Read the two introductions below and answer these questions.

1 Which introduction is formal?

2 Which features of informal writing can you identify in the informal introduction? Underline the features.

### Introduction 1

The aim of this paper is to evaluate the advantages and disadvantages of distance learning. Distance learning has fast become a popular alternative to attending university in person and most institutions now offer a number of courses online. It is, however, still inconclusive as to whether students who are taking these courses are as well served as those who still attend in person. This paper will look at issues around technology, work rate, and student–teacher contact to argue that the positives of distance learning far outweigh the negatives.

**Introduction 2**

In this essay, I will talk about the advantages and disadvantages of distance learning. Distance learning's getting more popular. More and more people choose distance learning over going to a uni in person, and most unis have loads of online courses. However, it's still a hot topic. People are unsure if students on DL courses receive the same quality of education as those going in person. In this essay, I will argue that the bad things are far bigger than the good things. I will look at technology, work rate and student–teacher contact.

**5b** Work in pairs. How can the informal introduction be made formal? Write down your ideas.

**5c** Correct the informal introduction using your ideas in 5b.

**5d** Read over your essay on distance learning and make it more formal.

# Unit 2  Communication

## Unit overview

| Part | This part will help you to … | By improving your ability to … |
|------|------------------------------|--------------------------------|
| **A** | **Follow lectures** | • use rising and falling intonation<br>• use pauses to improve comprehension<br>• prepare for lectures by predicting vocabulary. |
| **B** | **Recognize certainty in writing** | • understand how comment adverbs indicate degrees of certainty<br>• recognize how modal auxiliary verbs indicate certainty<br>• use adverbs of degree to emphasize meaning. |
| **C** | **Work effectively as a group** | • use questions to encourage participation<br>• check understanding<br>• choose between Past Simple and Present Perfect Simple. |
| **D** | **Deliver an academic presentation** | • use rhetorical questions<br>• use the phonemic alphabet. |
| **E** | **Paraphrase in writing** | • refer to an author's work<br>• use the Active or Passive to paraphrase<br>• change word forms and use synonyms to paraphrase. |

**Unit 2**

**Part A**

# Understanding spoken information

**By the end of Part A you will be able to:**

- use rising and falling intonation
- use pauses to improve comprehension
- prepare for lectures by predicting vocabulary.

## 1 Using rising and falling intonation

> When you listen to a lecture, *how* the lecturer expresses information can affect comprehension just as much as *what* they say.

**1a** Work in pairs. Discuss how the way someone speaks can affect listeners' understanding. Write notes below.

| Notes |
|---|
| *mispronounced words / strong accent = difficult to understand* |
| |
| |
| |
| |

2.1

**1b** Listen to an extract from a lecture on the ways in which listener understanding can be affected by how someone speaks. Does the lecturer mention all of your ideas from 1a? Do they mention any other factors? Make any changes or additions to the notes you made.

2.2

**1c** Listen to another extract from the lecture, which focuses on intonation. Answer these questions.

1 What is intonation?

2 How is a speaker's intonation important for the listener?

2.3

**1d** Listen to the extracts again, and complete this table.

| Is the lecturer … | Yes | No |
|---|---|---|
| **1** speaking too quickly/slowly? | | |
| **2** pausing after their main points? | | |
| **3** speaking with rises and falls in intonation? | | |
| **4** speaking in a flat tone? | | |

2.4

**1e** The lecturer mentioned that a rising (↑) or falling (↓) intonation to words in sentences can affect meaning, giving the example: 'Body language is really important for communication.' Listen to the sentence being spoken in three different ways. Match them with the possible meanings below.

1 Emphasizing a point.

2 Making a statement.

3 Questioning information.

**1f** Compare your answers with a partner.

**1g** Listen to a conversation between two students. Mark the words in bold with ↑ (rising tone) or ↓ (falling tone).

2.5

> **A:** What do you think the term 'body language' **means**?
> **B:** Body. Language. Can you **guess**?
> **A:** Hmm. Well, it must be about **bodies**, and **language**, and, language through your **body**, and …
> **B:** And … ?
> **A:** And, not through your **mouth**.
> **B:** Yes, that sounds right.

**1h** Work in pairs. Read the dialogue aloud using the correct intonation.

**1i** Complete these general rules with *rising* or *falling*.

1 With *wh*-questions the final word of the sentence usually has a _____ intonation.

2 With *yes/no* questions the final word of the sentence usually has a _____ intonation.

3 If someone is listing information, the content words usually have a _____ intonation to show that the speaker has not finished. The final word of the list usually has a _____ intonation, to show that the speaker has finished speaking.

## 2 Using pauses to improve comprehension

**2a** Work in pairs. Discuss reasons why people pause while they are speaking. Think about how pauses can help the listener. Write notes in the table below.

| Reasons for pauses in speech |
|---|
| *To show that the speaker is about to change topic* |

**2b** Listen to an extract from a lecture that explains how pausing can promote listener understanding. Does the lecturer mention all of your ideas from 2a? Do they mention any other factors? Make any changes or additions to the notes you made.

2.6

**2c** Listen again. Mark where the speaker makes a short pause (/) or a long pause (//).

> In its simplest form, pausing is used to give the speaker time to breathe. Used well, pausing can help focus the listeners' attention on important information. Pauses can be used to emphasize new or important vocabulary. Sometimes pauses are very short. Other times pauses are longer. Long pauses can signify that a new point will follow. Pauses can be used to give listeners and the speaker time to think. Pauses can also give students time to take notes.

**2d** Check your answers with a partner. Discuss why you think the speaker pauses where they do, and for the length of time they do.

**2e** Look at this extract from a lecture about body language. Mark the transcript where you think the speaker would pause. Mark short pauses (/) or longer pauses (//). Read the extract aloud to help you.

> In fact, there is some research which claims that the speaker's body language can be just as important as their choice of words. One researcher has claimed that as much as 55% of a message is carried through body language, with 38% carried through tone of voice, and only 7% transmitted verbally. So if a speaker does not engage with the audience by making eye contact, for example, or talks in a very flat tone, then they may fail to communicate anything, because their listeners switch off. So clearly it can be important, although how important depends on the situation. A little experiment you could all try is to watch a drama on TV with the sound turned off. How much of the story can you still understand?

2.7

**2f** Listen to the extract. Check your answers.

**2g** Work in pairs. Answer these questions.

1 Do you think that the pauses help you to identify and understand the main points of the lecture?

2 How else does the lecturer use their voice to help you understand the main points?

## 3 Preparing for lectures by predicting vocabulary

> Before attending a lecture, you should try to find out more about the topic by doing some background reading. Reading before a lecture helps you to learn key words, and build your understanding of the subject.

**3a** You are going to listen to a lecture with the title 'Is body language universal?' Work in pairs. Read the definition of body language and write down two points you think will be included in the lecture on universal body language.

*Body language is the movements or positions of your body that show other people how you are feeling, even though you do not tell them in words. For example, 'I could tell from her body language that she was very embarrassed.'*

1

2

> You should analyze the important words in the lecture title and try to predict some of the key words that may be used in the lecture. Doing this will mean that new or unfamiliar vocabulary is less likely to prevent you understanding.

**3b**  Write words with a similar meaning to *universal* (synonyms), and words with opposite meanings (antonyms) in the table below. Use a thesaurus to help you if necessary.

| Synonyms of *universal* | Antonyms of *universal* |
|---|---|
| global | local |
| | |

**3c**  Write more examples of body language and gestures and their meanings in this table.

| Body language and gestures | Meaning |
|---|---|
| smile | you are happy |
| wave | to say 'hello' |
| | |

**3d**  Compare your ideas with a partner. Discuss which of the examples of body language and gestures you think are more likely to be universal. Write *U* next to any example you think is universal.

2.8

**3e**  Listen to an extract from a lecture with the title 'Is body language universal?' Check whether the lecturer mentions your ideas in 3d.

**3f**  Listen again. Tick (✓) any words in the tables in 3b and 3c which the lecturer uses.

> When you listen to a lecture, you may not understand every word, even if you do prepare in advance. You can sometimes guess the meaning of a word from the words around it, or from what you have understood of the content so far. In other words, you can use the context to help you guess the meaning of words.

**3g**  Look at this extract from the lecture on body language. Underline any vocabulary that you don't understand.

> … Donald Brown, an anthropologist at UC Berkeley, identified a list of behaviours which he claimed are universal. These included behaviours to communicate shyness; facial expressions of disgust, fear and surprise …

**3h** Work in pairs. Try to guess the meaning of the words you underlined in 3g. Use the suggestions below to help you.

*Example*

*facial*

1 Think about the sound of the word. Does it remind you of another English word you know, related to the body? What form of the word is it likely to be?
2 Think about the words around it. What do you think a facial expression might be?

**3i** What do the words *disgust*, *fear* and *surprise* mean? What might they all be examples of (something that can be communicated with a facial expression)? Words in a list such as this are likely to be of a similar type.

Remember that you don't need to understand every word to understand the lecturer's main point. Do you need to know what *UC Berkeley* or *anthropologist* mean to understand the main point of the extract?

2.9

**3j** Listen again to part of the extract from the same lecture. As you listen, underline any words you don't understand.

The important lesson from this is that if you go to another country you mustn't think that people will automatically understand your gestures. In the worst case, you may insult someone by accident. But what of universality – the idea that there is a core of gestures which are so basic in their meaning, so human, that they are used and understood almost identically by every culture on the planet? Many things, such as smiles and frowns, are understood everywhere.

**3k** Work in pairs. Try to guess the meaning of the words you underlined in 3j by following the techniques above.

> If a word is essential to the main point of a lecture, the lecturer will probably repeat it more than once, use synonyms of the word, or simply explain it more fully.

2.10

**3l** Listen again to another part of the extract from the same lecture. Answer these questions.

1 What is the first gesture which the speaker mentions?
2 How does the speaker indicate that he is going to explain what this term means?

**3m** Work in small groups. Discuss your answers as a whole class.

**4 Listening for intonation and pauses**

**4a** You are going to listen to an extract from a lecture with the title 'Communication in the twenty-first century', comparing present-day communications technology with that of the 1970s. Work in small groups. Predict main points you think the lecturer might mention and any vocabulary and expressions you think he will use. Write your ideas below.

| Communication in the twenty-first century |
| --- |
|  |

2.11

**4b** Listen to the extract and answer these questions.

1 Were your ideas about possible content and language correct?

2 Did your brainstorming of ideas help you to understand the extract?

**4c** Listen to the extract again. Complete this table by ticking (✓) the correct column (*No* or *Yes*).

| Does the speaker ... | No | Yes |
| --- | --- | --- |
| **1** pause to emphasize new or unusual vocabulary? | | |
| **2** pause after the main points? | | |
| **3** use rising and falling intonation? | | |
| **4** use intonation to show they have (or have not) finished their main point? | | |
| **5** speak at a speed that helps students? | | |
| **6** explain new vocabulary? | | |

**4d** Read the transcript of the extract in 4b. Underline examples of the techniques from 4c. Number them 1–6.

People in the 1970s could only have dreamt of communicating through mobile phones, email, the Internet, not to mention Internet on your mobile phone. Modern technology would have seemed like the stuff of fantasy, of science-fiction. In those days, people would have been lucky to receive a message by snail mail – that's to say, through the post. Perhaps they would receive a telephone call from time to time, but communication took so much more time and effort. Yet, I ask you, was that such a bad thing? Isn't there something about opening up a letter that someone has spent time on, about seeing their handwriting, which makes it all so much more personal? Some people argue that it's more convenient to live in this modern technological age, a time where no one is ever unavailable, but I would suggest that it is less personal to live and to communicate in this era.

**4e** Work as a whole class. Discuss how successfully the lecturer used intonation and pauses to facilitate listener understanding.

## 5 Review and extension

### Using a thesaurus

A thesaurus can help you find synonyms and antonyms of vocabulary items. When you use a thesaurus, you have to be very careful that the synonym you choose matches the exact meaning of the word **in the context in which it is being used**. Understanding the form and meaning of the word you wish to replace will help you with this.

**5a** Work in pairs. For each of the sentence pairs below discuss what is wrong with the synonym in bold in the second sentence. What would be a better synonym choice? Use your thesaurus to help you.

**1 a** It is important for lecturers to **pause** from time to time (when they are talking).

   **b** It is important for lecturers to **silence** from time to time (when they are talking).

**2 a** When I asked her if she wanted a coffee, she **gestured** to say 'no'.

   **b** When I asked her if she wanted a coffee, she **signed** to say 'no'.

**3 a** Gestures which are widely understood in England may not be known **universally**.

   **b** Gestures which are widely understood in England may not be known **commonly**.

2.12

**5b** Listen to a short extract from a lecture on the media. First write your own notes. Then use your notes to complete these points (1–3).

> 1 *Recent research findings indicate …*
>
> 2 *Some difficulties in studying media use are due to …*
>
> 3 *People can afford to use new gadgets because …*

**5c** Listen to the extract again and underline in the transcript below any words you don't understand.

> One startling finding from the latest research is that three quarters of eleven-year-old children in developed countries have their own television, games console and mobile phone. But there are some difficulties in researching media use due to the way people of all ages combine different forms of the media in increasingly sophisticated ways. A teenager might listen to music while surfing the Internet, or listen to podcasts of favourite programmes. Certainly there is now much less need to watch TV programmes in real time, when they are all available via the Internet.
>
> What is noticeable about all these changes is the way people enjoy adopting and using new devices. It's hard to remember that twenty or thirty years ago mobile phones, even big ones, were just a science fiction fantasy for most people. In addition, the cost of all these services is steadily falling, so that price is no longer a real barrier, even for children. Of course, there are likely to be some important effects on society from all these changes, but that's a topic I need to discuss at another time.

**5d** Using the techniques in this Part try to guess the meaning of the words you underlined in 5c. Check your answers in a dictionary.

**5e** In the table below, write five words from the extract in 5c. Try to choose words which are unfamiliar to you. Use a thesaurus to find synonyms and antonyms of the words which could be used in the same context.

| Vocabulary | Synonyms | Antonyms |
| --- | --- | --- |
| *certainly* (adv.) | *indeed* (adv.)<br>*definitely* (adv.)<br>*of course* | *possibly* (adv.) |

**5f** Add these words to your personal vocabulary logbook.

# Understanding written information

**By the end of Part B you will be able to:**

- understand how comment adverbs indicate degrees of certainty
- recognize how modal auxiliary verbs indicate degrees of certainty
- use adverbs of degree to emphasize meaning.

## 1 Understanding how comment adverbs indicate degrees of certainty

Academic language used in written texts is typically more *cautious* and less *certain* than many other types of writing. Research is constantly taking place and understanding of subjects changes. It is also difficult to prove that something is definitely true. Academic writing therefore tends to use *hedging language*: academic texts use language which indicates the writer's opinions about the importance of the information they give, and how likely they think it is to be true.

***Examples***

***Importantly***, *trends in media use are changing.* (the writer thinks this is important)

***Clearly***, *trends in media use are changing.* (the writer is certain that the claim is true)

***Arguably***, *trends in media use are changing.* (the writer is cautious about whether the claim is true)

**1a** Read the extract below from an article about online information sources. Answer these questions.

**1** According to the writer, how reliable are online sources such as Wikipedia?

**2** What does the user's level of confidence in sites such as Wikipedia depend upon?

There is considerable debate about the reliability of collaborative sources of information online, such as blogs, newsgroups and sites such as Wikipedia. Significantly, a recent study found that the majority of people interviewed on the subject said that, while they frequently use blogs and wikis for information, their confidence in the reliability of these is low. Evidently, there is a problem of trust between users and contributors to such sites. However, the users' level of confidence presumably depends on the quality of the information available in the source, so it is necessary to find some means by which the quality of such sources can be guaranteed.

**1b** Work in pairs. Underline the comment adverbs in the extract. Write them in the appropriate place in this table.

| Purpose | Comment adverb |
| --- | --- |
| shows importance | |
| shows certainty | |
| shows caution/uncertainty | *apparently* |

**1c** Work in pairs. Write the comment adverbs in this list in the appropriate place in the table in 1b.

~~apparently~~    arguably    clearly    crucially    especially    naturally

obviously    possibly    potentially    undeniably    undoubtedly

**1d** Work in pairs. Answer the questions below about these statements (1–2).

   **1** *Undeniably, everyone finds email the most convenient way to communicate.*

   **a** Does *undeniably* mean it can be denied or it cannot be denied?

   **b** Do you think that this statement is true?

   **c** Is this statement cautious?

   **2** *Arguably, email is now the most important communication tool.*

   **a** Is this statement more or less cautious than the first one?

   **b** Could you argue that this statement is not true?

> The first sentence above is a generalization. It makes a strong claim about *everyone*, and therefore it is unlikely that it is, in fact, true. It is not a complete statement of the truth to the same extent that these sentences are:
>
> The Times *is an English newspaper.*
>
> *People can get news from a number of different sources.*

**1e** Work in pairs. Discuss why many writers tend to avoid using very certain comment adverbs like *undeniably* and *undoubtedly* in academic writing.

**1f** Read this extract from an article about the online encyclopaedia Wikipedia. According to the writer, what is Wikipedia's greatest weakness?

> Supporters of Wikipedia claim that the technological era has created access to information for all. Any contributor to Wikipedia may provide information in highly specialized fields. However, this strength is also arguably its greatest weakness. The fact that anyone can edit Wikipedia may make the contributions from experts less important.

**1g** Read the extract again and answer these questions.

    **1** Is the writer's personal opinion strong, or does the text seem to be quite cautious?

    **2** What comment adverb does the writer use?

    **3** Is this comment adverb cautious or certain?

> Comment adverbs are used to qualify the point being made. They usually refer to the whole sentence and are most often found at the beginning of the sentence but can be used in other positions.

**1h** Read this extract from a student essay about using the Internet for research. Underline five comment adverbs in the extract.

> Unquestionably, most students these days use the Internet to research their essays. Clearly, it is much more convenient than going to the library, and, naturally, students want the easiest option. Apparently, some students are distracted by email and other elements of the Internet when they are working at a computer. However, this is presumably true for those students who would be easily distracted anyway.

**1i** Work in pairs. Discuss whether the Internet is an advantage or disadvantage for students.

**1j** Write three sentences expressing your opinion on the discussion in 1i. Use a different comment adverb in each sentence to indicate how certain or cautious you are about your opinion.

*Example*
*The Internet has certainly transformed how students conduct research over the last twenty years.*

## 2  Recognizing how modal auxiliary verbs indicate certainty

**2a**  Read the student's essay below about the advantages and disadvantages of using Wikipedia as a research tool. Which of these paragraphs (1–3) best summarizes the writer's opinion?

1  There are many advantages to using Wikipedia, although some critics claim that Wikipedia cannot be trusted. However, Wikipedia is in fact very trustworthy because of its editing process, so it is actually suitable for academic work.

2  There is debate over the suitability of using Wikipedia for academic research. Because even non-experts can contribute to Wikipedia, critics claim that this makes Wikipedia unreliable. However, others claim that this is not a problem if Wikipedia has expert editors, and so if the quality of Wikipedia continues to improve, it should be considered a true encyclopaedia.

3  There are some positive aspects to Wikipedia. In particular, the fact that non-experts can contribute makes it more democratic. However, there are serious shortcomings because the information on Wikipedia is currently unreliable, so Wikipedia cannot be recommended for academic research.

In recent times, there has been much debate about the influence of Wikipedia in academic research. Many academics consider that Wikipedia is a good research tool, while others doubt its credibility. Although Wikipedia can be viewed as a good academic research tool, there are evidently some shortcomings.

Supporters of Wikipedia claim that the technological era has created access to information for all. As such, any contributor to Wikipedia may provide information in highly specialized fields, making the contributions from experts less important. However, they fail to acknowledge that one cannot be compared to an expert in a particular field merely by having access to information. For information to be considered reliable and authentic, it must come from someone who has spent much of their time studying a particular topic, making them an authority in their field.

On the other hand, people opposed to expert involvement in Wikipedia state that the editing process of Wikipedia provides up-to-the-minute information. They assert that this keeps the public well informed and that misinformation is regularly corrected. They suggest that if the editing procedure were expert, then expert writers might not be needed. Clearly, it seems that if experts edited the content, public opinion would still be heard, but only if it was reliable.

In conclusion, Wikipedia is naturally a good source of information, but obviously still needs to be improved by adding expert review procedures and contributions by other academics. This could improve quality. This essay strongly recommends that Wikipedia should be regarded by experts as a true encyclopaedia.

**2b**  Read the essay again and answer these questions.

1  How strong is the writer's opinion in this essay?

2  Which language highlights the writer's opinion?

3  Which language does the writer use to express caution about information?

> Modal verbs are another example of *hedging language*. They can be used in writing to show degrees of certainty and caution. They are often used in conjunction with comment adverbs.

**2c** Underline the modal verbs in the essay in 2a which show degrees of certainty or caution. Write them in the appropriate place in this table.

| More certain | More cautious |
| --- | --- |
| | *may* |

**2d** Read this extract from a student's essay. What are the writer's three main points?

*Naturally, the Internet is available to everyone in the UK today. As we all know, boys use the Internet more often than girls, and girls prefer to see their friends in person rather than sit at a computer emailing them. Obviously, British teenagers should become more active, because they prefer to play computer games than play sport.*

**2e** Work in pairs. Discuss these questions.

1 How certain is the writer about the points they are making?

2 Do you agree with the writer's opinions?

3 Can you think of any evidence which contradicts the writer's claims?

**2f** Rewrite the extract in 2d to make it more cautious. Use hedging language (modal verbs and comment adverbs) where appropriate.

## 3 Using adverbs of degree to emphasize meaning

**3a** Read the extract below from a journal article. Decide if the writer will agree or disagree with this statement in the rest of the article: *The Internet has significantly improved communication in the last twenty years.*

[1] These days, we are accustomed to think of the Internet as being 'completely open for both business and home users' (D'Emanuele, 1995, p.68). [2] The Internet is an enormously powerful method of communicating. [3] It provides information on almost any subject, and is available to anyone with the technology needed to access it. [4] Originally, however, the Internet was developed for a somewhat different purpose: it was still intended for communication, but it was developed by scientists, and was nearly unknown outside of the academic community.

**3b** Read the extract in 3a again and answer these questions.

1 Which section(s) (1–4) support the statement that the Internet has significantly improved communication in the last twenty years, and which section(s) do not?

2 To what extent does the writer agree with these statements?

a Now, the Internet is open for both business and home users.

b Information on any subject can be found on the Internet.

**c** When it was first created, the Internet was unknown outside of the academic community.

---

Adverbs of degree help the writer to comment on the *completeness* and *scale* of things. You can use adverbs of degree to emphasize:

**1** completeness
*We are accustomed to think of the Internet as being '**completely** open for both business and home users'.*

**2** near completeness
*It provides information on **almost** any subject …*

**3** lack of completeness
*The Internet was developed for a **somewhat** different purpose …*

**4** scale or size.
*The Internet is an **enormously** powerful method of communicating.*

---

**3c** Work in pairs. Write the adverbs of degree in this list in the appropriate place in the table below.

almost    completely    enormously    extremely    ~~fully~~    hugely    partially

somewhat    thoroughly    totally    utterly    very    wholly

| Emphasis | Adverb of degree |
|---|---|
| completeness | *fully* |
| near completeness | |
| lack of completeness | |
| scale or size | |

**3d** Read another extract from the journal article and underline the adverbs of degree. Write them in the appropriate place in the table in 3c.

As for worldwide access, many researchers believe that in the next ten to fifteen years, nearly everyone in the world will be able to get online in one way or another. Yet it should be remembered that the Internet is still massively biased towards English speakers. Users of the Internet still need to be somewhat proficient in English, as virtually all of the content online is carried in that language. In this respect, and despite easy technical access, the language barrier means that much of the Internet still might not be entirely accessible to all.

**3e** Underline the adverbs in these sentences. For each sentence, decide which word the adverb modifies.

*Example*
*The Internet has proved to be <u>extremely</u> useful.* (*extremely* modifies *useful*)

1 The Internet was partially developed by a US government research programme.
2 Experts predict that increasing numbers of people will choose to do things such as shopping and enjoying entertainment wholly online.
3 Current internet speeds in many countries cannot fully satisfy consumer demand for internet access.
4 The existence of the Internet is likely to be hugely important in the coming century.
5 Recent years have seen a very rapid growth in the number of companies doing business online.
6 Improvements in technology will mean that more people can get online very easily.

---

The adverb *very* is used to modify adjectives and adverbs, but not verbs.
*Example*
*Cost can make access to the Internet **very expensive**.*
NOT *Cost ~~very restricts~~ access to the Internet in developing nations.*

You can use **very much** as an adverb of degree to emphasize verbs.
*Example*
*Cost **very much restricts** access to the Internet in developing nations.*

---

**3f** Work in pairs. Find and correct a mistake with *very / very much* in one of these sentences.

1 The majority of people surveyed claim that they very much enjoy the convenience of internet access.
2 Different users have very much different demands on the network.
3 It is very unlikely that internet capacity will be able to increase much more.
4 The development of the internet very much improved global communications in the late 20th century.

**3g** Read the extract from an article about internet access on p.71. What claims does the writer make about:

1 the importance of the Internet?
2 the effect that the Internet has had on business?
3 the effect that the Internet has had on everyday life?
4 people's expectations of instant access to information?

Since its origins in the late 20th century, the Internet has revolutionized personal, business and official communications. Routine business communications are now almost wholly conducted via email or online conferencing, and it is impossible to imagine a return to a pre-Internet system of doing business, with its inevitable delays and requirements for face-to-face meetings. Similarly, it is no exaggeration to say that the Internet has completely transformed both the lives of private individuals, and the way in which they see the world. The expectation of instant communication and the ability to access information on virtually any topic – either through a computer terminal or mobile device – is now very much taken for granted. Indeed, an entire generation has now grown up which never knew the pre-Internet world. It is likely that future generations will be somewhat puzzled by the idea of a world without the convenience that the Internet offers.

**3h** Underline any adverbs of degree that you find. Work in pairs. How do they alter the meaning?

**3i** Work in pairs. Discuss the extent to which you agree with the writer's claims.

> **LESSON TASK**  **4 Expressing opinions**

**4a** Work in pairs. Discuss whether you agree with this statement. Give reasons.

*Because of computer technology, teenagers are becoming increasingly antisocial.*

**4b** The statement in 4a is the subject of a seminar discussion. Work in groups of four. One pair will argue for the statement, and one pair will argue against.

Before you start, read the essay below and find arguments to support your position in the debate. Decide whether the arguments are based more on opinion or fact.

Many adults argue that adolescents are becoming more antisocial because of computer technology. They criticize teenagers for sitting at a computer all day instead of going out and talking with their friends face-to-face. This essay will suggest reasons why this may be a valid argument, but will also give examples of how computer technology might make certain teenagers more sociable.

Evidently, the very nature of a computer is antisocial. People who sit at a computer hour-upon-hour will be isolated and may not have any real-life interaction. Moreover, Smith (2005) reports that playing computer games can be addictive; the more you sit at a computer playing games, the less you want to do anything else. Some people suggest that you do not need the real world when you have a virtual world, and teenagers are less likely to make the effort to maintain real friendships if they have virtual playmates.

Nevertheless, computer technology can really help teenagers who live far from their friends, or those who do not like to socialize, perhaps because they are shy. Teenagers can play computer games with their friends who live in other towns, whilst talking to them through a headset. And, crucially, shy people can make friends through the monitored use of approved social networking sites. Jenkins (2007) highlights that the Internet can improve the social lives of some of the shyest teenagers, and help them to make new friends.

In conclusion, a controlled use of the Internet can help teenagers to become more sociable, so long as there is balance, and the use of computer games does not become an addiction.

**4c** Prepare notes for the debate. Use evidence from the text in 4b to support your claims. Prepare to use adverbs of degree, comment adverbs and modal auxiliary verbs to indicate the strength of your opinion.

> **'Because of computer technology, teenagers are becoming increasingly antisocial.'**

**4d** Work in groups of four to discuss the statement. Try to make sure that when you make claims, you express them using an appropriate amount of caution.

**4e** After the discussion, work with members of your group and discuss these points.

    **1** Which pair presented the most effective argument during the discussion? Why?

    **2** What specific examples of claims put forward in your discussion can you remember that you felt used cautious language well?

    **3** Which claims can you remember that might be improved? How?

## 5   Review and extension

**5a** Read this extract from a report on how children use the media. According to the writer:

    **1** what types of activity would British children prefer to do, if possible?

    **2** what impact do parents have on the amount of time that British children spend indoors?

    **3** what impact does the development of new forms of media have on the time that British children spend indoors?

### How children use the media

A year-long study of media use by British children (6–17 years) has found that although they spend more time indoors using the Internet or watching TV than children in other countries, this is not always their choice. Their preference may be for outdoor activities, but for various reasons this may not be possible.

The study indicates that 99% of children watch television, on average for 2½ hours a day. Over 80% also watch DVDs and videos regularly. Computer games are also popular, with over two-thirds of children playing them. Nearly 90% also listen to music, but this is often while doing something else, such as homework. More than half read non-school books, with many reading an hour each day.

The reason why these activities are so popular seems to be that parents are worried about safety outdoors, and that there is also a lack of places where children can go locally. This appears to be especially true of older children (over 11) who are less likely to attend organized leisure activities. It is interesting to compare this with the situation in other European countries; for example only 34% of German and 21% of Swiss children complain that there is nothing to do locally, while in Britain the figure is 81% among 15 year-olds. Significantly, when parents are asked about their concerns for their children, only 11% said that their neighbourhood was 'safe', although 56% thought that the streets where they had grown up were safe. The same parents listed fear of illegal drugs and crime as the main dangers their children faced. It appears, then, that these parents create media-rich home environments as a compensation for these perceived threats.

It was found that more than half the homes had cable or satellite television, thus providing children with channels offering dedicated programmes aimed at young people, such as cartoons. Large numbers of children were found to have their own personal stereo, TV and computer. Compared with other European countries, British children have far more screen media entertainment.

Despite this, the study suggests that given a choice, children prefer being outdoors with friends. Watching TV was widely considered as a second-best option, for when you were bored or tired. When asked to choose activities for an ideal day, 39% of children chose meeting friends and 35% playing sport, whereas watching television was only selected by 14%.

It appears, then, that although children in the UK have access to far more media than children in other countries, their use of this is partly a reflection of their parents' fears rather than their own choice.

**5b** Underline any language in the text in 5a that indicates the strength of the author's opinion.

**5c** Write a brief essay (200 words) discussing the statement you debated in the lesson task. Use your notes from the debate and the language from this Part.

'Because of computer technology, teenagers are becoming increasingly antisocial.'

# Investigating

**By the end of Part C you will be able to:**

- use questions to encourage participation
- check understanding
- choose between Past Simple and Present Perfect Simple.

## 1 Using questions to encourage participation

> Using questions effectively can help to promote effective group work and ensure that everyone in the group participates. During group discussions, you may need to ask questions to find out other people's ideas and opinions, ask others to explain their ideas more fully, check that you have understood something or help with group administration (e.g. move on to another point, distribute roles, etc.).

**1a** Answer these questions.

**1** Have you ever done a group presentation?

_____

**2** Why do you think people like group work?

_____

**1b** Which question in 1a is a:

**1** *wh*-question? _____

**2** *yes/no* question? _____

> **Wh-questions**
>
> You can use these words to make *wh*-questions: *what, who, when, where, whose, whom, why, which* and *how*. They are used to ask for different kinds of information.
>
> The usual form of *wh*-questions is:
>
> *Wh*-question word + auxiliary/modal verb + subject + main verb.
>
> Auxiliary verbs such as *be, do* and *have* are used in various forms depending on the tense.
>
> **Examples**
>
> *What _____ your most memorable experience of group work?*
>
> *When _____ you last work in a group?*
>
> *Where _____ you studied before?*
>
> Sometimes, *wh*-questions are used to find out more about the subject of the verb. For this type of question, an auxiliary verb is not used, and the *wh*-word comes before the verb.
>
> **Example**
>
> *Who got the highest score in the last assessment?*

> **Yes/no questions**
>
> *Yes/no* questions anticipate an answer of *yes* or *no*. They are formed like *wh*-questions but without the question word.
>
> **Examples**
>
> _____ *he proficient at using PowerPoint? Yes, he is.*
>
> _____ *study at your house tomorrow? No, you can't, I'm afraid.*

**1c**  Complete the examples in the box above using a suitable auxiliary or modal verb. There may be more than one possible answer.

**1d**  Work in pairs. Ask and answer these questions.

**1** Do you have any experience of group work?

**2** What don't you like about group work?

**1e**  Which questions in 1d encouraged longer/shorter answers?

> Questions that require brief answers, often just *yes* or *no*, are sometimes referred to as *closed questions*, and questions that require a fuller response as *open questions*. Both kinds of question can be useful in a group discussion.

**1f**  Work in pairs. Think of two examples of closed questions and two examples of open questions, then ask each other your questions and give appropriate answers.

Now discuss these points.

**1** Which type of question encouraged the respondent to think more?

**2** Which type of question gave more control to the person who asked it?

**3** Which types of question would be most suitable for doing these things in a group discussion?

- Asking for somebody's opinion on a topic.
- Checking if you have understood what somebody else has said.
- Asking for a fuller explanation of something.
- Asking if it is all right to move on to a different point.

2.13

**1g**  Listen to three students meeting for the first time to establish rules for their research and to assign roles to each member of the team. Answer these questions.

**1** Were they successful in establishing rules and assigning roles? Why / why not?

**2** Did each group member participate equally? Why / why not?

**1h**  Read this transcript of the discussion and underline the questions.

**Chris:** OK, so our group has to research how students use communication technology for their studies and then give a ten-minute presentation next month. As this is our first meeting, let's introduce ourselves properly. As you know, my name's Chris. OK, let's see, how much group work have we all done before? Personally, I've done plenty of group work before. Have either of you got experience of group work?

**Alice:** I have a little.

**Fareg:** Yes, quite a lot.

**Chris:** Alice, have you had any positive experiences of group work?

**Alice:** Yes, mostly.

**Chris:** Mostly? What didn't you like about it?

**Alice:** Well, my last group wasn't very organized, so we got behind in our preparation and …

**Chris:** So, do you mean it wasn't very successful?

**Alice:** Yes, I do.

**Chris:** Fareg, were your experiences of group work positive?

**Fareg:** Yes.

**Chris:** Uh huh. What was good about it?

**Fareg:** Well, I've done a fair amount of group work, and generally speaking I think it goes well most of the time. Of course you need to compromise sometimes: you don't always get your own way, but working together you can achieve things which are better than working alone, and that's a nice feeling.

**Chris:** Have you never had a bad experience?

**Fareg:** No.

**Chris:** Good. Well, let's see who should do what. Who would like to be co-ordinator? Actually, I think I would. Is that OK with everyone?

**Alice:** Yes.

**Fareg:** Sure.

**Chris:** Good, we're agreed. Now, rules. What rules should we introduce?

[Silence]

**Chris:** Alice, what rules should we introduce?

**Alice:** Sorry, I don't know what you mean. What kind of rules are you talking about?

**Chris:** Well, for instance, I think we should meet every two days to discuss what work we've all done, so our next meeting would be on Thursday. OK?

**Alice:** Sure, no problem. What time should we meet?

**Chris:** I don't mind. You decide, Alice.

**Alice:** Oh, any time's good for me.

**Chris:** Well, it's up to you.

**Alice:** Really, any time's fine.

**Fareg:** OK, look. Is two o'clock a good time for everyone?

**Alice:** Yeah, that's fine.

**Chris:** That's good for me too. So, what other rules should we have?

**Alice:** Oh, I see. Well, I think we should meet in a coffee shop every two days, as it's more relaxing. It's much better working there than in the library. We should do that; it would be fun!

**Chris:** I meant, what rules we should create so that we all work hard and make sure that we are organized. Oh, never mind, I'll type some rules up and then email them to you.

**1i** For each of the questions you have underlined, identify and label them as either *closed* questions (C) or *open* questions (O).

**1j** Circle the correct words in bold in these sentences.

   1 An open question can help make the **questioner** / **respondent** feel involved.

   2 An **open** / **closed** question can help to include someone who is quiet.

   3 *Wh*-questions are usually **open** / **closed** questions.

   4 One problem with **open** / **closed** questions is that the respondent may lose focus and talk about something off-topic, especially if the phrasing of the question is obscure.

   5 A closed question is likely to receive a **long** / **short** answer.

   6 A closed question tends to give control of the conversation to the **questioner** / **respondent**.

   7 *Yes/no* questions are usually **open** / **closed** questions.

   8 A closed question is **good** / **bad** for checking simple facts.

   9 A closed question is **good** / **bad** at encouraging more detailed responses.

**1k** Work in pairs. Read the questions you underlined in the transcript in 1h again. Discuss which questions limited communication in this group discussion, and why this might have been the case.

**1l** Rephrase the questions which limited communication so that they improve the communication within the group.

## 2 Checking understanding

2.14

**2a** Listen to two new students discussing their first research project. Answer these questions.

   1 What do they need to do?

   2 How do they decide to do this?

**2b** Listen again. Write expressions that you hear in the correct column of this table.

| Asking someone to repeat/ explain something | Checking that you've understood | Checking that someone has understood you |
|---|---|---|
| | *Does that mean we need to …?* | |
| | | |

**2c** Work in pairs. Add any other expressions you can think of to the table.

**2d** Work in small groups. Discuss what you have learned about how to participate effectively in group work. Ask questions and check your understanding.

## 3 Choosing between Past Simple and Present Perfect Simple

> You will use past tenses in group discussions or tutorials:
> • to discuss previous experiences or study
> • to discuss research that has been done
> • to refer to comments that group members made previously.

**3a** Read the pairs of sentences below and do these tasks.

    **1** Underline the verb forms and identify the tenses used in each sentence.

    **2** Discuss and explain why you think different tenses have been used in each pair of sentences.

    **1 a** The service launched last week is already very popular.

      **b** The other services that have been launched already are very popular.

    **2 a** The government released a report on new media use last week.

      **b** Online news websites have been extremely successful.

    **3 a** The BBC launched its 'iPlayer' service in 2007.

      **b** Many TV stations have started parallel broadcasting services online.

**3b** Work in pairs. Discuss when to use the Past Simple and the Present Perfect Simple. Use the example sentences in 3a to help you.

**3c** Write *Past Simple* and *Present Perfect Simple* in the correct place in this table.

| Tense | Refers to |
|---|---|
| | • specific times (*yesterday, last week*) |
| | • completed events in the past |
| | • recent events at non-specific times (*already, just*) |
| | • events that continue up to the present (*so far, up to now*) |
| | • past events that are still relevant in the present |

**2.15**

**3d** Listen to an extract from a lecture about media use. How are TV viewing trends changing?

**3e** Read the transcript of the extract and underline all the examples of Past Simple and Present Perfect Simple. Decide why the tense was used in each case, using the table in 3c to help you.

Today I'll be looking at the effect that the growth of online media is having on TV viewing habits – that's regular TV viewed through a TV set. So, just a few years ago, there was basically no online TV capability on the Internet. But that's been changing rapidly over the last few years, and now we have already reached the stage where most major TV companies also offer parallel online TV services. So, in just a few years, we have gone from zero internet TV to an almost total availability of TV online.

Now, how is this changing the way that people watch TV? Is it changing it in fact? Well, the speed of this development meant that, so far, only one or two studies have been done on this, and they didn't reveal much change. However, last year there was another study completed in Reading which found that there are significant changes in the way people now choose to get access to TV. Unsurprisingly, they found that increasing numbers of people have started to rely on online TV services rather than regular TV broadcasts. It's easy to understand why, as well: with broadcast TV you have a fixed schedule and either need to watch a show at the appointed time, or record it; otherwise you're going to miss it. But with online TV, the viewer can watch a show on demand, almost any time they like, and this means that fewer and fewer people have been watching regular broadcasts, in favour of online TV. So we can see that there has been a significant shift in viewing habits over the last few years.

**3f** Complete these sentences using the Past Simple or Present Perfect Simple form of the verbs in brackets.

*Example*
*The Arabic news station Al Jazeera <u>has recently launched</u> (recently/launch) its online service.*

1 So far, online news channels _____ (*be*) very popular.

2 As Katie _____ (*already/say*), we need to meet regularly to discuss our ideas.

3 Recent reports claim that a large percentage of the population _____ (*not watch*) any online TV in the last year.

4 March 2008 _____ (*be*) the last time that the network suffered a failure of its website.

5 As media groups _____ (*say*) the last time this was discussed, there is a need for better service from TV channels online.

**3g** Compare your answers in 3f with a partner.

**4 Working in a group**

**4a** Work in pairs. Your tutor will assign one of the tasks below to your pair. Follow the instructions on the card carefully because afterwards you will be having a group meeting with other students doing the same task.

---

### Task A

*You have been given this research task by your tutor.*

***In the next tutorial, you will run a group seminar discussion on how students use communication technology for their studies. Research the topic fully beforehand. You will be expected to use both printed academic sources and your own experience to inform your discussion.***

*Your group is meeting today for the first time to discuss the task. During this initial meeting you need to:*

- *ensure that everyone understands the task*
- *assign roles for the members of the group (co-ordinator, presenter, lead researcher, slide designer)*
- *brainstorm some ideas on the topic*
- *discuss each member's previous experience of using communication technology for their studies.*

*In your discussion try to use open and closed questions, and check your understanding using appropriate expressions.*

---

### Task B

*You have been given this research task by your tutor.*

***In the next tutorial, you will run a group seminar discussion on whether children and young teenagers should have access to the Internet. Research the topic fully beforehand. You will be expected to use both printed academic sources and your own experience to inform your discussion.***

*Your group is meeting today for the first time to discuss the task. During this initial meeting you need to:*

- *ensure that everyone understands the task*
- *assign roles for the members of the group (co-ordinator, presenter, lead researcher, slide designer)*
- *brainstorm some ideas on the topic*
- *discuss each member's previous experience of using the Internet when they were younger.*

*In your discussion try to use open and closed questions, and check your understanding using appropriate expressions.*

**4b** You will be observing a group discussing one of the tasks in 4a. As you observe, make notes on the language the group members used. Afterwards, use your notes to give feedback to the discussion group members.

| Did the group … | Yes/No | Examples |
|---|---|---|
| 1 fulfil the requirements of the task? | | |
| 2 ensure that everyone spoke? How? | | |
| 3 use the Past Simple / Present Perfect Simple appropriately? | | |
| 4 use questions effectively? | | |

## 5  Review and extension

### The Past Simple: regular and irregular verbs

**5a** Read the extract below in which a student discusses a specific memory of group work. Answer these questions.

1 When did the group work discussed in the extract take place?

2 Is the group work complete now?

3 Does the extract suggest the student had mostly a positive or negative experience?

Last month my class had to give group presentations, so I spent a lot of time beforehand working on my presentation with three other classmates. Our teacher permitted us to choose our own group members, so that made it somewhat easier as we already knew each other. We met often to discuss our research. At each meeting, we organized what we were each going to do before we met again. Everyone was quite motivated and, in comparison with other groups in our class, communicated well and achieved a good result in the end. I think it helped that we knew we relied on each other in order to do well. It was hard work, but I learned a lot about myself in the process.

> To form the Past Simple for regular verbs, add *-ed* to the base form of a verb.
>
> ***Example***
>
> *talk → talked*
>
> There are, however, many irregular verbs.

**5b** Underline the verbs in the Past Simple in the text in 5a and add them to the example column of this table.

| Verb ending: | To make Past Simple | Example |
| --- | --- | --- |
| *-e* | Add the letter 'd' | create – created |
| consonant + *y* | Change 'y' to 'i' and add 'ed' | comply – complied |
| single vowel + single consonant | Double the consonant and add 'ed' | pat – patted |
| Other | Mostly add 'ed'; some irregular verbs | toil – toiled |

**5c** Add two more verbs you know to each of the verb types in the table in 5b.

### Error correction: Past Simple and Present Perfect Simple

**5d** This magazine article contains six errors using the Present Perfect Simple and Past Simple forms of the verbs. Underline the errors in the text and then complete the table on p.83.

The term 'blog' was first used in 1999 by Peter Merholz, who has borrowed the word from 'weblog'. Since then, use of the word has continued to spread in popularity, and is now a common part of an internet user's vocabulary. Thousands of blogging websites were created, but the blog world's innovators deserve credit for the online phenomenon's current success. In the late 1990s, sites such as LiveJournal (1999) and Open Diary (1998) introduced users to blogging, before they were replaced by the now popular Blogger and Blogspot along with millions of independent blogs created by users from all over the world. In 2007, a blog search engine called Technorati has claimed it had over 112 million blogs in its database. Since then, experts say, that number grew rapidly as access to new technology and easier blogging platforms became available. In the early days, blogs were primarily used by internet enthusiasts to provide personal commentary or serve as online diaries. However, over the past decade blogs expanded to include a wide range of ideas and functions, such as news, photography, videos, music and online radio, among others. Blogging has been such a success, one can only imagine where the world of blogging will take us next.

| Error | Reason why incorrect | Correction |
|---|---|---|
| *... who has borrowed the word from 'weblog'* | *Should be past simple as used with a specific date, 'in 1999'* | *... who borrowed the word from 'weblog'* |
| | | |

**Past experiences of group work**

**5e** Think of one of your past experiences of group work and consider the factors that made it successful and/or unsuccessful. Write notes in this table to prepare for a discussion about group work.

| Group work | Explanation |
|---|---|
| When and where; purpose of the group work | |
| Factors that made it successful | |
| Factors that made it unsuccessful | |
| Suggestions for future group work | |

**5f** Work in groups. Discuss your past experiences of group work using your notes in 5e.

# Reporting in speech

**By the end of Part D you will be able to:**

- use rhetorical questions
- use the phonemic alphabet.

> It is important for presenters to try to connect with their audience.
> For example, they should use techniques that make the audience feel involved,
> such as rhetorical questions. The presenter must also ensure that the audience
> understands what they say, for example by pronouncing key words clearly
> and correctly.

## 1 Using rhetorical questions

2.16

**1a** Listen to the introduction to a presentation. What is the speaker's opinion about approaches to presenting?

**1b** Listen again and answer these questions.

1 What question does the speaker ask?

2 Who answers the question?

3 How does asking this question help the presenter connect with the audience?

4 Does the speaker assume that most people have or have not given a presentation before?

> The speaker uses a *rhetorical question*. This is a question that the speaker uses
> when they do not expect the listener(s) to reply, but to consider the question in
> their mind.

**1c** Work in pairs. Discuss the effects that using rhetorical questions in presentations might have on the audience. Write your ideas in this table.

| Some effects of using rhetorical questions in a presentation |
| --- |
|  |

2.17

**1d** Listen to the next extract from the same presentation. Complete the transcript with the rhetorical questions the speaker uses.

**Nadeem:** Thanks, Sarah. As Sarah has just said, reading from a script is not the best way to present. _____
_____[1] Well, sometimes they do, but you'll notice that we aren't. That's because reading from a script means that a speaker can't engage well with the audience. How can we maintain eye contact if we're reading? More to the point, _____
_____[2] You probably wouldn't be able to hear a word I was saying. Next, Sarah will discuss this some more.

**Sarah:** Well, thanks Nadeem. So, reading aloud doesn't help a presenter's body language, or help to make their voice audible. Another important point is that when you read aloud from a script, you may not fully concentrate on what you're saying, making the word stress and intonation really unnatural. This, again, may lose audience interest. Plus, _____
_____[3] So, if we speak how we write, it would sound really artificial – that's to say, unnatural. But, _____
_____[4] _____
_____[5]

**1e** Work in pairs. Write the questions from 1d in the correct place in the third column of this table.

| Rhetorical question type | Form | Example |
|---|---|---|
| Question tag | Positive comment with negative question tag OR negative comment with positive question tag | |
| *Should …?* | *Should* + subject + verb | |
| Positive closed question | Auxiliary verb + subject | |
| Negative closed question | Auxiliary verb + *n't* + subject | |

**1f** Read the transcript in 1d again. How would you respond to each rhetorical question?

**1g** Match the rhetorical question types (1–4) with the predicted audience responses (a–d) and add any further ideas you have.

| Rhetorical question type | Predicted audience response |
|---|---|
| **1** Question tag | **a** To make the audience feel responsible/obliged due to the use of the modal verb, and think 'yes'. |
| **2** *Should …?* | **b** To give a negative response: 'no!' |
| **3** Positive closed question | **c** To agree with the comment, either 'yes' or 'no'. |
| **4** Negative closed question | **d** To give a positive response: 'yes!' |

**1h** Read this transcript from the final extract from the presentation. Write an appropriate rhetorical question in each gap.

> **Nadeem:** Well, as Sarah has already pointed out, reading aloud may seem easier, but _____
>
> _____[1]. (*question whether reading aloud sounds natural: Audience response should be 'no'*) Importantly, if you were to read from a script, it wouldn't convince me that you really knew much about your presentation topic. So, if you suffer from nerves, it's better to have note cards that can prompt your memory than a whole script that may make it sound like you don't really know what you're talking about! Reading aloud at home may be one effective way to practise your English pronunciation, but it certainly won't help you in a presentation.
>
> **Sarah:** So, to conclude this presentation, we'd like to suggest that we all try to present just by using notes and not a full script. As Nadeem and I have pointed out, it makes a presentation more convincing and engaging for the audience. _____
>
> _____[2]. (*question whether audience is in agreement: Audience response should be 'yes'*)

2.18

**1i** Listen to the extract and compare your answers.

**1j** Work in pairs. Discuss these questions.

1 Are the rhetorical questions you wrote as effective as the ones used by the speaker? Why / why not?
2 Is it possible to use too many rhetorical questions? What would be the effect on the audience of using too many?

## 2 Using the phonemic alphabet

**2a** Write down some methods for learning how to pronounce new words.

| Ways to learn how to pronounce new words |
| --- |
| |

**2b** Compare your answers with a partner. Discuss the possible advantages and disadvantages of each method.

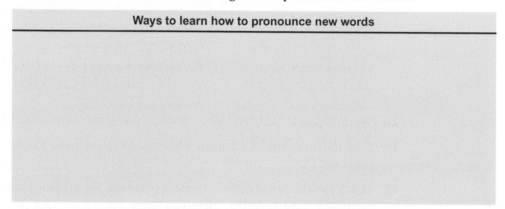

> One reliable method of learning and recording the pronunciation of vocabulary is to use a phonemic alphabet (see **Appendix 2**). A *phoneme* is a symbol used to record an individual sound. Some phonemes look the same as letters of the alphabet, but many are different. Slash symbols [/] are always used with the phonemic alphabet to make it clear that it's the pronunciation not the spelling of

alphabet is especially useful with the English language, because the spelling of words rarely matches the pronunciation.

***Example***
*I could hear my heart beat.*
  /hɪə/    /hɑːt//biːt/

**2c** Look at the words *hear, heart* and *beat*. How is *ea* pronounced in each word?

2.19

**2d** Listen and check your answers to 2c. Practise saying the words aloud.

**2e** There are three phonemes in the word *heart*. Work in pairs and try to identify the three individual sounds.

> Using the phonemic alphabet, the pronunciation of *heart* is written: /hɑːt/. The three phonemes in heart are /h/, /ɑː/ and /t/.
>
> The pronunciation of some words may vary due to a speaker's accent. The phonemic alphabet can be used to record any pronunciation. This lesson will use the standard British English pronunciation.

**2f** How many phonemes, or individual sounds, are in the word *could*? Try saying the word aloud to help you. Remember that a phoneme is different from a syllable.

**2g** Read the text, where a student discusses his experience of giving a presentation. What was his main problem?

> When I was first asked to give a presentation at university, I had no idea what to do. I didn't really know the subject so I had to do a lot of extra reading. I made lots of notes and tried to include everything in my presentation. Before the big day, I practised in front of my friend, in front of the mirror; I even went to sleep dreaming of my presentation.
>
> When the day finally came, I was so nervous and it got worse because I had to wait ages for other people to finish. When it was my turn, I could hear my heart beat, but when I started talking I stopped feeling so nervous. The waiting was much more difficult than actually presenting. I was quite well prepared but I talked for too long. One of the most difficult things for me was deciding what to leave out. But when I finished I felt pretty good and I gained confidence, not only in giving presentations, but in the knowledge of my subject, too.

**2h** Work in pairs. Complete the table on p.88 with the words from the box. Use a dictionary to help you.

> when /wen/    first /fɜːst/    pretty /prɪti/    report /rɪpɔːt/    plan /plæn/
> bring /brɪŋ/    was /wɒz/    presentation /prezənteɪʃən/    talk /tɔːk/    bit /bɪt/
> specific /spəsɪfɪk/    think /θɪŋk/    should /ʃʊd/    very /veri/    about /əbaʊt/

| Words with 3 phonemes | Words with 4 phonemes | Words with 5 or more phonemes |
|---|---|---|
| | | |
| | | |

**2i** Words have syllables as well as phonemes. Say the words in the box. How many syllables do the words have?

***Example***

*presentation* has four syllables: pres|en|ta|tion

NOTE: A word may have a different number of syllables and phonemes; for example, presentation has four syllables and eleven phonemes.

2.20

**2j** In the extract in 2g, the student uses the noun *presentation*. Listen and answer these questions.

   **1** Is the stress on the second or third syllable?

   **2** There are two sounds represented by the letter e in the word *presentation*. Are they pronounced the same way?

### Identifying the schwa sound

> The *e* sound used in the second syllable of the noun *presentation* is represented by the phonemic symbol /ə/. This sound is the most common sound in the English language. It is so common that it has been given a name – schwa. Knowing how and when to use the schwa will help spoken English to sound more natural.
>
> Any vowel letter in a word could be pronounced as a schwa, but it is only used in an unstressed syllable.
>
> ***Examples***
> *about   specific   pencil   proposal   suggest*

2.21

**2k** Listen to the examples above to hear the schwa sound.

**2l** Work in pairs. Practise saying the words in 2k aloud using the schwa sound.

**2m** Read these two extracts from the presentation in 1a and 1d and underline places where you think the schwa is.

   **1** Nadeem and I will be discussing some of the differences between speaking with only the assistance of brief notes in presentations, and simply reading aloud from a script.

   **2** As Sarah has just said, reading from a script is not the best way to present. But, don't many people present that way?

2.22

**2n** Work in pairs. Listen to the sentences to check your answers to 2m. Then answer these questions.

   **1** What do you notice about many of the words that contain a schwa: are they content or function words (refer back to Unit 1 Part A)?

   **2** How does the use of the schwa in unstressed words make it easier for the listener to understand each sentence?

2.23

**2o** Listen to this sentence again. Underline where you can hear the schwa sound.

> Nadeem – and – I – will – be – discussing – some – of – the – differences – between – speaking – with – only – the – assistance – of – brief – notes – in – presentations – and – simply – reading – aloud – from – a – script.

**2p** Work in pairs. Discuss whether you marked more schwa sounds in 2m or 2o. Was it easier to understand the sentence in 2m or 2o?

> ➤ **LESSON TASK**   **3 Giving a short presentation**

**3a** You are going to give a section of a presentation to another pair of students about 'The advantages and disadvantages of using the Internet to help students learn English pronunciation'. The presentation should last for a maximum of five minutes.

You will only present main advantages and disadvantages, not the introduction or conclusion. Begin your presentation with the words '*… and now we will focus on some of the advantages and disadvantages of learning pronunciation online*'. One student will present the advantages and the other student will present the disadvantages.

Work in pairs. Prepare your presentation using information from the extracts below, along with ideas from your own experience. If you are unsure of the pronunciation of any vocabulary, check the correct pronunciation in a dictionary before you begin to speak.

Try to use rhetorical questions and the schwa sound.

Use notes, but do not write a complete script.

### Havard, N. (2010):

Computer technology can be a huge advantage for second language learners, and their tutors, as it encourages autonomy (Ashmore, 2009), and, today, students have a vast range of choice of computer programs to assist their linguistic development. This could be particularly advantageous for students wishing to improve their pronunciation. There are several free online dictionaries of English pronunciation, but some are limited in the number of words they contain. Pronunciation software can be of use to students wishing to improve at the sentence-level, but may be expensive for individuals to purchase. Many colleges have begun to acquire this facility, but students are often required to make use of it in public areas, which could lead to embarrassment and reluctance to take part. If students wish to have their own speech analyzed, and not to just listen-and-repeat sounds, they are still reliant on their teachers, as no suitable computer program has currently been produced.

### Zheng, F. (2009):

As a learner of English, I used to struggle to distinguish certain sounds, particularly the schwa sound in grammatical words such as *for* and *the* when they are spoken in sentences. I wouldn't think about the sound of the sentence, just the sound of the individual words. I don't think that my use of online dictionaries helped me with that, as it only considered words out of context. What I did find useful was recording myself speaking and then listening to it back. It didn't have anything to do with a computer, but I could hear myself where my problems lay, which then taught me what I needed to improve.

**3b** Work in groups of four. Take turns to give your presentation. As one pair speaks, the other pair writes notes in this table.

| Did the pair ... | Yes/No | Examples |
|---|---|---|
| **1** use rhetorical questions effectively? | | |
| **2** use information from the texts as well as their own experience? | | |
| **3** pronounce content words clearly and correctly? | | |
| **4** mispronounce any words? | | |
| **5** use the schwa sound appropriately, especially with function words? | | |
| **6** do anything else well/poorly that deserves comment? | | |

## 4 Review and extension

### Recognizing phonemic signs

**4a** Read this transcript of the introduction to a presentation. What is the subject of the presentation?

> Good morning everyone, and thank you for making time to come to this presentation today. Today I'll be looking at what holds second language learners back from speaking English, and offer various techniques to overcome this. You've heard people say they can understand English, but they can't speak it, haven't you? Why do you think that is? Three reasons could be nerves, translating from the first language, and not having the opportunity to practise. In the next hour, I'll present some solutions, and take any questions you may have on the subject at the end.

**4b** Underline on the transcript in 4a where you expect to hear schwa sounds.

**4c** Listen to check if your predictions were correct.

2.24

> There are over 40 phonemic symbols used to represent English sounds, and of those, 21 represent vowel sounds. Vowel sounds are separated into three types: short vowels (such as the schwa), long vowels (such as /ɑː/ in the word *heart*) and diphthongs (such as /aɪ/ in the word *high*).

| Sound | Examples | Your examples |
|---|---|---|
| Short vowel sounds | | |
| /ɪ/ | him, will, sit | |
| /ɒ/ | on, what, lot | |
| Long vowel sounds | | |
| /iː/ | feet, heat, seat | |
| /ɜː/ | learn, bird, turn | |
| /uː/ | true, blue, flew | |
| Diphthongs | | |
| /aɪ/ | high, try, fly | |

2.25

**4d** Listen and repeat the words in the second column of the table above. Add more examples of words containing these sounds to the table.

**4e** Find examples of the sounds in the table above in the extract in 4a. Write the words in the table.

**4f** Listen to the extract in 4c again. Were your answers in 4e correct?

> Learn more about the phonemic alphabet by searching online or looking in books. Some key words to help you are: International Phonetic Alphabet; pronunciation; phonemic symbols.

**4g** In your *Skills for Study* course you have been studying how young people obtain news. From your research, you will have found some important words that you may find difficult to pronounce. Add the words to this table, and then write the words in phonetic script using what you know and a dictionary to help you.

| Vocabulary from *Skills for Study* course | Phonemic transcription |
|---|---|
| **1** media | /miːdɪə/ |
| **2** | |
| **3** | |
| **4** | |
| **5** | |
| **6** | |
| **7** | |
| **8** | |
| **9** | |
| **10** | |

> Whenever you find a new vocabulary item, particularly one you find difficult to pronounce, you should include the phonemic transcription alongside the word in your vocabulary logbook.

# Reporting in writing

**By the end of Part E you will be able to:**

- refer to an author's work
- use the Active or Passive to paraphrase
- change word forms and use synonyms to paraphrase.

## 1 Referring to an author's work

**1a** Read the extract about referring to another author's work in academic writing. Answer these questions.

1 Who do you think is the audience for this text?

2 What are the two methods of referring to authors' work mentioned in the text?

3 Which method uses an author's idea(s) and not their exact words?

---

When preparing to write an essay, it is important to conduct research by reading sources on the subject. Making notes on any useful information in such sources as academic text books, journals and websites will help you to both consolidate and develop their ideas on the topic. However, if this information and ideas are to be used in your essay, you must acknowledge that you have found them in another writer's work. You can do this in two ways. The first option is to use a quotation and 'quote' some of the information you have found. To do this, you need to copy the author's exact words, and acknowledge these with the use of quotation marks before and after them, together with a citation (the author's name, date of the publication, etc.). A second option when using another writer's ideas is to 'paraphrase' or 'summarize' the useful information from the source by changing the language, but, most importantly, still maintaining the original ideas. Again, it is necessary to cite the author. It is also important to note that when changing the language of the original text, it isn't enough to simply change some of the vocabulary. To paraphrase effectively you may also need to change the structure of the original sentences and show that you fully understand the ideas you are using.

Ashmore, C. (2010). *Making Reference in Academic Writing*.
Brighton: Terrace Publishing

---

**1b** Work in pairs. Discuss why it is important, in academic writing, to paraphrase and not only use quotations. Write your ideas below. Then discuss your answers with the whole class.

| Why is it important to paraphrase authors' ideas and arguments in academic writing? |
| --- |
| |

**1c** Listen to an extract from a lecture on academic writing and check your ideas. Add to your notes where necessary.

2.26

## 2 Using the Active or Passive to paraphrase

> To paraphrase effectively, even in note form, you must understand the full *meaning* of the language you wish to paraphrase. If you do not fully understand what you have read, it will be impossible to convey the precise meaning in your own words.

**2a** Work in pairs. Using your own words, explain what this extract from 1a means.

> To paraphrase effectively you may also need to change the structure of the original sentences and show that you fully understand the ideas you are using.
>
> Ashmore, C. (2010)

**2b** Read the paraphrases below and identify what has been done to each sentence to change it from the original in 2a. Decide whether any of the sentences successfully paraphrase the original sentence.

1 In order to demonstrate an understanding of the sources you have read, Ashmore (2010) states that ideas should be paraphrased through altering the organization of the sentences written by the author.

2 There are a number of different elements to effective paraphrasing. According to Ashmore (2010), altering sentence structure is one of these aspects.

3 To demonstrate that ideas have been comprehended, ideas should be paraphrased through using different methods. Ashmore (2010) claims that amending sentence structure is a valuable way of paraphrasing.

**2c** Label sentences a and b with the *subject, verb, object* and *agent*.

> **a Active:** *Students should change the structure of the original sentences.*
> **b Passive:** *The structure of the original sentences should be changed by students.*

Then answer these questions.

1 Is the meaning of sentences a and b different?

2 What is the action in both sentences? Who does the action?

**2d** Use what you know about the difference between active and passive sentences to decide on the best answer from the alternatives given.

1 The object of an active sentence corresponds to the **object / subject** of a passive sentence.

2 Only active sentences that have a subject, verb and **object / agent** can be put into the passive voice.

3 In active sentences, the subject and the agent are **the same / different**. In passive sentences the subject and the agent are **the same / different**.

4 Passive sentences do not always have an agent. However, if the agent is given in a passive sentence, it usually follows the word **with / by**.

**2e** Work in pairs. Study the sentence pairs and match the effect of changing the sentences from active to passive with the effects in the table.

1 **a** The newspaper made a mistake when they reported the incident.

   **b** A mistake was made when the incident was reported.

**2 a** I have found that most people use the Internet for more than an hour a day.

   **b** It has been found that most people use the Internet for more than an hour a day.

**3 a** Fewer people are watching the news.

   **b** The news is being watched by fewer people.

| Effect of changing from Active to Passive | Example sentence |
|---|---|
| Makes findings seem more generally accepted | |
| Removes blame | |
| Shifts the focus to the person/thing receiving the action | |
| Shows objectivity (it becomes less personal) | |

---

You form the passive with the correct form of *to be* + past participle.

*Example*

*Some news websites **are visited** by millions of people every day.*

---

**2f** Identify the active sentence and the passive sentence in these sentence pairs.

   **1 a** Ten years ago, radio presenters read the news.

     **b** The news was read by radio presenters ten years ago.

   **2 a** Not much news is read by young people.

     **b** Young people do not read much news.

   **3 a** Modern media has changed the way people read the news.

     **b** The way people read the news has been changed by modern media.

   **4 a** Young people are watching news on specialized websites.

     **b** The news is being watched by young people on specialized websites.

   **5 a** We should question the reliability of citizen journalism.

     **b** The reliability of citizen journalism should be questioned.

**2g** Complete this table using the passive sentences in 2f to help you.

| Tense | Form |
|---|---|
| Present Simple | |
| Present Continuous | *am/are/is being* + past participle |
| Past Simple | |
| Present Perfect | |
| with modal auxiliary verbs | |

**2h** Change these active sentences into passive sentences using the table in 2g.

*Example*
*Some older people do not use the Internet.*
*The Internet is not used by some older people.*

**1** Social networking sites have revolutionized the way people communicate.

_____

**2** Teenagers are playing more online video games.

_____

**3** People didn't use video calling in the past because of high costs and poor quality.

_____

**4** Many people consider the influence of social networking sites to be quite positive.

_____

**2i** Check your answers with a partner.

## 3 Changing word forms and using synonyms to paraphrase

> Although many language changes need to be made when paraphrasing, technical vocabulary is very unlikely to be changed and often remains as part of the paraphrase. This is because subject-related vocabulary usually has a highly specific meaning and rarely has accurate synonyms. Examples of technical vocabulary for different subjects are:
>
> Business – *human resources, company, marketing, sales, etc.*
> Chemical sciences – *mass, molecules, experiment, reaction, etc.*

**3a** Work in pairs. Read the sentence below and answer these questions.

**1** What technical language is used in the sentence?

**2** Which words can you paraphrase?

The Prime Minister has promised to provide access to the Internet for less affluent members of society.

**3b** Work in pairs. Think of synonyms for these words.

| Original words | Synonyms |
| --- | --- |
| promise | |
| provide access | |
| affluent | |

**3c** Rewrite the sentence in 3a using synonyms. Remember to keep the technical vocabulary used in the original sentence.

**Original sentence**
The Prime Minister has promised to provide access to the Internet for less affluent members of society.

**Paraphrase**

**3d**  Answer these questions about your paraphrase in 3c.

    **1** Does it retain the meaning of the original sentence?

    **2** Has enough of the language been changed?

    **3** Is it a complete and grammatically correct sentence?

> It is not always possible to change active sentences into the passive. It can be enough to paraphrase by changing the word order, word form and vocabulary.

**3e**  Complete the paraphrase using another form of the words in bold in the original extract.

> According to a recent **statement** by government representatives, there is to be **an increase** in access to the Internet. This is particularly important given that seventy-five per cent of people interviewed recently felt that to have a fulfilling life without the Internet is **impossible**. It was found that, without **access** to the Internet, some people can feel isolated. **(Seabrook, 2009)**

Seabrook (2009) reports how, in 2009, government representatives _____[1] that there was to be _____[2] access to the Internet. Research found that seventy-five per cent of interviewees felt that it was an _____[3] to live a fulfilling life without the Internet. Furthermore, it was suggested that if the Internet was not _____[4], it could be isolating for some people (ibid.).

**3f**  Work in pairs. Rewrite the paraphrase in 3e to improve it. Replace some of the non-technical words with synonyms and make other changes where possible.

## ▶ LESSON TASK   **4 Paraphrasing information**

**4a**  This extract from a piece of research by Robert Watkins (2010) has been used by three writers to inform their answer to this essay question: *Discuss the factors that make communications technology popular.*

Work in small groups. Read the text and underline any vocabulary you do not understand. Discuss the meaning of the text as a whole and try to guess what any unknown words may mean from the context.

> The results of our survey indicate that people aged 30–39 most commonly use the Internet to buy commodities and to organize leisure time activities, whereas people aged 18–29 report that communicating with loved ones is their main motivation for connecting to the Internet. Advances in communications technology that improve convenience and reachability are awaited by all those questioned, yet equal numbers welcome and fear the imminent prospect of video calling.

**4b** Read the three paragraphs below, which have paraphrased information from the extract in 4a. Work in pairs. Discuss the strengths and weaknesses of each paragraph. Rank the paragraphs in order of most effective to least effective (in terms of quality of paraphrasing). Be prepared to justify your decision.

**A**

Convenience is a factor that makes modern communications technology popular. It is now possible to shop online, organize activities for any free time, and easily communicate with others. The Internet saves people time and effort. Watkins (2010) says that people aged 18–29 use the Internet to communicate with loved ones, whereas people aged 30–39 use it to buy commodities and organize free time. People seem to like the idea of reachability, but, according to Watkins (2010), fear the prospect of video calling.

**B**

*Convenience is a significant factor that makes modern communications technology popular. Watkins' (2010) survey highlights that, of those questioned, everyone is eager to find new technology that makes life more convenient, and, moreover, that makes people more reachable. The survey highlights communication with friends and family as the main motivator for people in their late teens and twenties to use the Internet (Watkins, 2010). However, technology that uses a video link may be too much of an invasion of privacy, with half of the people surveyed stating that video calling is something to be feared (ibid.).*

**C**

People aged 18–29 report that communicating with loved ones is their main motivation for connecting to the Internet (Watkins, 2010). Modern communications technology is especially convenient when living a long distance away from family and friends. People look forward to technological advances that improve convenience and reachability, yet equal numbers of people questioned in their research welcome and fear the idea of video calling (Watkins, 2010).

**4c** You are going to use information from the following extract from an academic text to write a paragraph in answer to the question: *What are the effects of spam on communication?* Work in small groups.

**1** Decide which information from the passage can be used to support your ideas on this topic.

**2** Write a paragraph that responds to the question and paraphrases relevant information from the extract to support your ideas.

While spam is still an enormous time waster, the amount of time dealing with it seems to be decreasing. Respondents reported spending six per cent of their communication time dealing with spam (last year's number was seven per cent). For internet users, this amounts to more than five workdays per year assuming daily use for 50 weeks out of the year. The decrease in time dealing with spam while browsing the Internet went from eight per cent in 2004 down to 0.1% in 2005, which may be due to the improvement of spam preventive technology (e.g. advertisement filter, pop-up blockers) embedded in the newest browsers. The figure for respondents who reported 'having used the Internet that day' was higher – twelve minutes per day (two minutes less than the previous year), or about nine days per year, assuming daily use for 50 weeks. Clearly there are significant productivity consequences of dealing with spam and computer problems.

**Kedwood, R.** (2009). *Efficient User Guidelines*. New York: King Street Press

**4d** Work with another group. Compare your paragraphs and decide which is the best, giving reasons why.

## 5  Review and extension

### Using the Active and Passive

**5a** Complete this table with the correct version of the active or passive.

| Tense | Active | Passive |
|---|---|---|
| Present Simple | All our first-year students use this book. | This book is used by all our first-year students. |
| Present Continuous | All our first-year students are using this book. | 1 |
| Past Simple | In the past, all our first-year students used this book. | 2 In the past … |
| Past Continuous | 3 Before the new edition came out, … | Before the new edition came out, this book was being used by all our first-year students. |
| Present Perfect Simple | 4 <br> … since 2009. | This book has been used by all our first-year students since 2009. |
| Present Perfect Continuous | All our first-year students have been using this book for quite a few years now. | NOT USED |
| Past Perfect Simple | Up until last year, all our first-year students had used this book. | 5 Up until last year … |

| | | |
|---|---|---|
| Past Perfect Continuous | *Up until last year, all our first-year students had been using this book.* | NOT USED |
| Future | **6** *Next year …* | *Next year this book will be used by all our first-year students.* |
| Future Continuous | *Over the next few years, all our first-year students will be using this book.* | NOT USED |
| Future Perfect | *By the end of next term, all our first-year students will have used this book.* | **7** *By the end of next term, …* |
| Future Perfect Continuous | *By the time it gets to Easter, all our first-year students will have been using this book for two terms.* | NOT USED |

**5b** Complete this text using the correct form of the verbs in brackets.

    **1** Identify a suitable tense. There may be more than one possible answer.

    **2** Decide if the verb in brackets should be in the active or passive voice.

What do people do when they communicate online? In recent years many studies *have been conducted* (conduct) to explore computing habits. One recent study _____[1] (show) that communication with friends, relatives or colleagues _____[2] (take up) the largest portion (39%) of internet communication time. The use of email, instant messaging or chat rooms _____[3] (include) in this figure. The second largest percentage of online communication time _____[4] (relate) to playing games. In comparison with last year, the time spent playing games _____[5] (double).

Although the Internet _____[6] (make) interpersonal communication incredibly efficient and convenient, studies also show some of its downsides. Six per cent of time _____[7] (eat up) by dealing with spam. This is an issue that needs to be addressed in the future, especially by employers. The time given to work-related communication online (5%) _____[8] (rank) below the time spent dealing with spam, which could _____[9] (improve) by an up-to-date security system.

**5c** You are going to write a paragraph in answer to the question: *Modern technology is better for communication than more traditional methods. Do you agree or disagree?*

Read the two texts on p.100 and make notes on the ideas that you could use to support your answer.

Even for those who are up to speed with technology, the very nature of modern communications may prove unappealing. Email, instant messaging and social networking may make communication quicker, but is there any soul? Innovations, such as blogs, enable us to communicate with a virtual community of strangers. Social networking encourages many to share both meaningless and meaningful activities with 'friends' who may never be seen in person. Yes, all this communication is quick, and easy. Yes, it is convenient. But, it is also disposable and forgettable. Handwritten letters, postcards, telephone conversations, may take time and effort, but it is that effort that makes this kind of communication significant. Modern communications are supposed to help people make the best use of their time, but taking time to communicate meaningfully is what people will value in the future.

(Doherty, 2010)

We cannot exaggerate the advantages of using the Internet for communication. Access to the Internet gives power through the knowledge it contains. Most people accept that the Internet provides hope for developing countries, as easy communication and access to information may provide assistance with health care, education, and even the economy. Internet access for all may be a few years away, but it could be life-changing. Think back to a world without the Internet. Without the Internet, there was no easy way to share knowledge. Communication was time-consuming and unreliable. A secure internet connection results in high-speed communication and access to the latest information, which could help to make the world a more aware and connected community.

(Jones, 2010)

| Notes |
| --- |
| 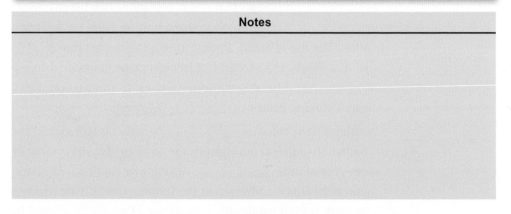 |

**5d** Write a paragraph of around 250 words in answer to the question: *Modern technology is better for communication than more traditional methods. Do you agree or disagree?*

Remember to:

• paraphrase information from the sources to support your answer
• use reporting verbs (refer back to Unit 1 Part D) to indicate your opinion when paraphrasing

   *Example*
   *Jones (2010) asserts that …*

• use formal language
• give both sides of the argument to show that you have considered all possible views.

# Unit 3 Science and technology in society

## Unit overview

| Part | This part will help you to … | By improving your ability to … |
|------|------------------------------|-------------------------------|
| **A** | **Understand lectures** | • notice signpost words and phrases<br>• predict and identify key words in context<br>• identify cause and effect linking words and arguments. |
| **B** | **Understand and use academic texts** | • identify key vocabulary<br>• use prepositional phrases<br>• express possibility. |
| **C** | **Understand sources and develop coherence in your writing** | • recognize your reading level<br>• use synonyms<br>• understand substitution. |
| **D** | **Give an academic presentation** | • use signpost words and phrases in presentations<br>• deal with questions<br>• use intonation to maintain interest<br>• refer to visual materials. |
| **E** | **Use information from sources** | • report ideas from sources<br>• summarize information from other sources<br>• integrate information from sources into writing. |

# Understanding spoken information

**By the end of Part A you will be able to:**

- notice signpost words and phrases
- predict and identify key words in context
- identify cause and effect linking words and arguments.

## 1  Noticing signpost words and phrases

> To really understand a text or a lecture, it is necessary to know topic-specific vocabulary. However, it is also important to pay attention to non-topic-specific vocabulary, as this can help in comprehending the development of ideas.

**1a**  Read this paragraph from an academic text. According to the author, which is worst:

**a** an earthquake?

**b** a drought?

**c** a flood?

> There have been many natural disasters which have had a major impact on social and political life. The newspapers tend to concentrate on those disasters which have the most serious loss of life, such as earthquakes, or those which provide the most dramatic headlines and personal stories, such as major floods. The media often ignore the real killer on the list – drought – which over the long term has a far more devastating effect on communities.

> It is possible to answer the question in 1a without fully understanding the topic-specific vocabulary (flood, earthquake and drought). The phrase 'the real killer' tells you the next item will be the most significant. In this example, the use of dashes (–) also indicates which natural disaster is the most serious, as it adds emphasis.

**1b**  Work in pairs. Discuss any negative effects that weather or climate change have had on your community or a community you know about.

3.1

**1c**  Listen to an extract from a lecture about the ancient city of Angkor. As you listen, write notes in the table on p.103.

| Angkor |
|---|
| Original theory about the disappearance of the population: |
| |
| Current thinking: |
| |
| Evidence for new theory: |
| |

**1d** Work in pairs. Listen again and each read one of the students' notes below. Tick (✓) anything that is correct, and change anything that is wrong.

| Student A | Student B |
|---|---|
| Angkor | Angkor |
| Theory 1 – declined because of conflict. | Conflict caused the decline in Angkor Wat, Buckley argues invasion from Siam caused it. |
| Theory 2 – Columbia University – Buckley – weather caused the decline. | Study of tree rings in wet years shows that the climate was cool. |
| evidence: ~~triringdater~~ (??) tree rings! | People and trees lived over a thousand years in Angkor, from 1400. |
| Suggests severe drout (??) in early 1400s (water supplies dried up) – not possible to prove though. | This helped the invasion. |

**1e** Check your answers with a partner. Discuss which of the students in 1d has a better understanding of the lecture.

**1f** Complete the transcript of the extract on p.104 using the phrases (a–g).

    **a** It's a way of

    **b** has cast doubt on this theory

    **c** ~~there has been some debate about~~

    **d** people have suggested that it was because of

    **e** they argue that a more likely explanation is

    **f** So that suggests, though of course this can't be proved, that

    **g** that gave them the data that they wanted

As you know, _there has been some debate about_ the causes of the periods of conflict in South-East Asia during the fifteenth and eighteenth centuries. The Cambodian city of Angkor, for example, was virtually abandoned at this time, and _____[1] an invasion from Siam, as Thailand was then called. But some recent research, and I do mean recent, _____[2]. A team from Columbia University, led by Brendan Buckley – that's B-U-C-K-L-E-Y – have looked at weather patterns in the region, and _____[3] a long drought, when monsoon rainfall was well below normal.

Unfortunately, there are no weather records for this period, so the team has had to use tree ring data. Are you all clear about what that is? _____[4] studying the rate of growth of certain trees by looking at the width of the annual rings; so in a wet year the trees grow more than in a dry one. Actually, it's more difficult in that region than in colder climates, because there's a wider range of tree species. However, they did find a type of conifer which can live for over a thousand years, and _____[5]: Vietnam and Thailand had experienced a severe drought in the early 1400s. _____[6] Angkor's decline was caused by its water supplies drying up, not by an invasion.

**1g** Listen again and check your answers.

**1h** You are going to listen to an extract from the first part of a lecture about synthetic genetics (creating artificial DNA in a laboratory). Work in groups. Discuss what you think are the ethical concerns about creating DNA artificially in a laboratory.

3.2

**1i** Listen to the extract. What are the two possible ways of controlling the development of artificial DNA technology?

**1j** Work in pairs. Listen again and each read one of the students' notes. Tick (✓) anything that is correct, and change anything that is wrong.

| Student A | Student B |
|---|---|
| 'Creating life' on your laptop – ethical questions | Responses to ethical questions raised by genetics: |
| 1 – make information available on Internet – on YouTube and Yahoo | 1) make information freely available – e.g. computer industry model – positive benefits but also viruses |
| 2 – ban research – like other forms of biological study | 2) ban new information – not likely outside state control |
| Need to 'unlearn' what we already know to stop new viruses like computer viruses developing. | Experts – prefer 1st option – creates people able to fix problems. |
| | How to co-ordinate and monitor development of new diseases? |

**1k** Check your answers with a partner.

**11** Listen again and underline the phrases in the transcript which the lecturer uses to signpost what they are talking about. Then write the phrases in the table.

OK. Right. Let's get started. <u>Well, you'll remember that last week</u> we were looking at some of the moral and ethical questions that limit research into genetics, particularly now with the development of synthetic genetics. Many people, including the scientists themselves, have worries about the role science could play in the creation of life. It will be a while before new life forms are created on someone's laptop, but this will come, and we need to be prepared.

Well, today we're going to explore this topic further and look at possible responses to those concerns that we discussed. One option is to make genetic information freely available to anyone. We've seen from the computer industry that an open approach allows individuals to develop their own ideas in spectacular new ways. Some of the most popular computer and internet applications, such as YouTube, Facebook and Yahoo, started off as very small-scale, home-grown projects. However, the same process that created these internet giants also produced thousands of computer viruses. So whilst an open approach might help address people's fears about artificial DNA technology, there are also concerns that unregulated research – that's research without government controls – could produce biological viruses with very real dangers.

A much more cautious option would be to ban the research now, while it's still very new, and the information is available to a very limited number of people. This has worked for other forms of biological study, but these tend to work only where the scientists are already working for governments.

Perhaps surprisingly, those who have given the topic some thought tend to favour the first option. They argue that once something has been learned, it is almost impossible to 'unlearn' it again. Instead it makes sense to be open to the new technology so we can take advantage of the benefits it may bring. The industry can take clear steps to protect itself as well, so that if a problem does occur, just as in the case of computer viruses, there are experts there to fix it.

Now we're going to focus on the challenges of co-ordinating a system to monitor the development of new diseases on an international level.

| Signposting | |
| --- | --- |
| **Function** | **Example** |
| Introducing the general topic | *The theme of today's lecture is …*<br><br>1 _____ |
| Reminding students about previous lectures | *Well, we're halfway through our programme on …*<br>*As you know, …*<br>*This reinforces the point I made earlier …*<br><br>2 _____ |
| Giving examples | *This is clearly illustrated by …*<br>*A good example of this is …*<br><br>3 _____ |

| | |
|---|---|
| Suggesting an approach | *People have thought that ...*<br>*One way of approaching this problem ...*<br>4 _____<br>5 _____ |
| Limiting the topic | *Well, we won't be addressing ...*<br>6 _____ |
| Questioning a view | *This may well lead to problems ...*<br>*... has cast doubt on this theory*<br>7 _____ |

> Keep several pages of your vocabulary logbook specifically for recording these 'signpost' phrases. They will help you to follow the meaning of lectures, and you will need to use them when you give a presentation yourself.

## 2 Predicting and identifying key words in context

> In lectures, speakers tend to group words together into 'chunks', with each chunk having one or two key words. The chunks are usually separated by pauses. It is often possible to predict what the key words will be in each chunk either from what the speaker has said before or through your own knowledge of the topic. If you can predict what will be said, this will make listening much easier.

### Identifying chunks

**2a** Work in pairs. Identify three chunks in this sentence and mark the pauses between them //.

> There have been a few developments particularly in the last five years that have transformed our understanding.

3.3

**2b** Listen to the sentence and check your answers.

**2c** Work in pairs. Predict what you think the chunks will be in this extract from the lecture on genetics in Section 1. Mark the pauses between them //.

> One option is to make genetic information freely available to anyone. We've seen from the computer industry that an open approach allows individuals to develop their own ideas in spectacular new ways. Some of the most popular computer and internet applications, such as YouTube, Facebook and Yahoo, started off as very small-scale home-grown projects. However, the same process that created these internet giants also produced thousands of computer viruses. So whilst an open approach might help address people's fears about artificial DNA technology, there are also concerns that unregulated research, that's research without government controls, could produce biological viruses with very real dangers.

3.4

**2d** Listen to the extract and check your predictions.

> When people listen, they pick up key words such as content words or important signpost words and predict what will be said next. This happens without thinking in our own language, but in another language we need to actively listen to identify the key words and make helpful predictions.

**2e** Underline the key content words in each chunk in the transcript in 2c.

**Example**

*One option // is to make genetic information // freely available to anyone.*

**2f** Check your answers with a partner.

**2g** You are going to listen to some short extracts from a lecture on introducing modern technology and farming techniques to farmers in the developing world. Work in small groups. Discuss these questions.

1 What do you understand by the term *green revolution*?

2 What examples of modern farming technology can you think of?

3 What do you know about how successful modern farming techniques are?

4 Are these techniques good for the environment? Why / why not?

**2h** The table below lists key words and phrases related to the lecture topic. Work in pairs. Try to predict some more key words which you would expect to hear in the extracts. Write them in the table.

| Modern farming techniques in the developing world | |
|---|---|
| developing world | poor crop yields |
| European | research |
| food production | scientists |
| methods of farming | small African farms |
| | |

3.5

**2i** Listen to the first extract and tick (✓) the words in 2h you hear.

**2j** Work in pairs. Summarize the general meaning of the extract using the key words you heard to help you.

**2k** Listen again and check your answers.

**2l** Work in pairs. Predict what you think the speaker will talk about (1–3) in the next extract.

1 Traditional farming methods used in small African farms

2 Some techniques associated with European methods of farming

3 The problems farmers in Africa have

**2m** Listen and check your answers.

**2n** Work in pairs. Write any new key words and phrases that you heard in the table in 2h.

**2o** Listen again and check your answers.

**2p** Work in small groups. Predict what you think the speaker will talk about in the last extract. Use the information you heard in the first two extracts to inform your predictions.

**2q** Listen and check your answers.

## 3 Identifying cause and effect linking words and arguments

**3a** Work in small groups. Discuss what you think the main causes of the following situations might be. What might the effects be?

1 In the UK the number of cars on the roads increased by more than ten million between 1990 and 2010.

2 There has been an increase in the number of children suffering from obesity in many developed nations.

3 There has been a sharp rise in the price of petrol over the last five years.

**3b** The words and phrases in bold in these extracts from a report on private car usage indicate cause and effect. What is the cause and what is the effect in each extract?

*Example*

*cause*          *effect*

*The number of cars on the road increased sharply*. **As a result**, *many governments tightened the driving laws*.

1 Petrol prices in many countries are increasing, **so** car manufacturers have begun to develop electric or hybrid cars.

2 Parking cars in city centres is becoming more difficult and expensive. **Therefore** more people are starting to use public transport when going to work.

3 Air pollution in some cities is at dangerous levels **due to** exhaust fumes from increased traffic levels.

4 Cities like London have introduced traffic congestion charges for private cars, **thereby** encouraging more people to use public transport.

5 Some drivers share cars with other people when driving to work **because of** the increase in fuel prices.

6 Some cities have developed extensive underground transport systems. **Consequently**, movement around these places is generally much more efficient.

**3c**  Write the words in bold from 3b in the correct place in the table.

| Introduces effect | Introduces cause |
|---|---|
| *as a result (2)* | |

> A lot of university work involves identifying and assessing the causes and effects of phenomena. Use your vocabulary logbook to keep a note of cause and effect expressions that you encounter.

**3d**  Work in pairs. Which of the words and phrases in the table in 3c

**1** are used to link cause and effect as part of the same sentence?

**2** are used to link cause and effect in two different sentences?

Write 1 or 2 next to each phrase in the table.

**3e**  You are going to listen to an extract from a lecture about research into the eating habits of rats, which involved manipulating their diet and monitoring the effects. Work in pairs. Complete these sentences choosing the most likely ending (a or b).

*Example*
*Scientists have been studying the eating habits of rats. As a result,*
**a**  *we now understand more about the addictive nature of junk food.*
**b**  *we now have a more complex relationship with food.*

**1** A diet of junk food produced addictive behaviour in rats. Consequently,
  **a** they chose to eat healthy food.
  **b** they always chose to eat junk food when given a choice of diet.

**2** Over time, the rats stopped responding to the pleasures of junk food. As a result,
  **a** they needed more food to satisfy their hunger.
  **b** they ate more healthy food.

**3** Rats and humans share a large amount of DNA. Therefore
  **a** similar effects might be expected in humans.
  **b** humans will become addicted to junk food if they eat too much.

**3f** Listen to the extract and check your answers.

3.8

**3g** Listen again and write down the linking words you hear which introduce the causes and effects in 3e.

> **LESSON TASK**    **4 Developing arguments in speaking**

**4a** Work in pairs and discuss these questions.

    **1** Has air travel become safer or more dangerous in recent years?

    **2** What changes have been made to make air travel safer?

**4b** Listen to extracts from two lectures, explaining some of the reasons for improvements in flight safety. As you listen, make notes in the table below on why air travel has improved and the effects the improvements have had.

3.9

| Why is air travel safer? | Effects |
| --- | --- |
|  |  |

**4c** Compare your notes in small groups. Discuss what you think the major factor in this improvement in safety has been.

**4d** You will give a two-minute talk on improvements in flight safety. Follow these instructions.

    **1** Use the information in 4b and 4c to decide on your arguments.

    **2** Look back in the unit at ways of developing your arguments.

    **3** Plan what you will say and how you will develop your ideas.

**4e** In pairs or small groups, give your two-minute talk. While other students are speaking, think about how effectively they develop their ideas. Give them feedback when they have finished.

## 5 Review and extension

Complete the following extract from a lecture on science and libel laws using appropriate signposting words and phrases from the list.

**1** ... *cast doubt on these claims* ...

**2** ... *there are concerns that* ...

**3** *Today we're going to develop this topic and* ...

**4** *This reinforces the point I made earlier that* ...

**5** *This is clearly illustrated by* ...

_Well, you'll remember that_ last week we were looking at how science is viewed by the general public. Those scientists who do try to enter the public sphere are often criticized by their fellow scientists for seeking 'celebrity' status. _____ᵃ look at other possible risks of entering public debate.

Recently, some scientists have found themselves victims of libel laws. These laws are supposed to prevent lies being written in the media, but can cause problems. _____ᵇ the case of Simon Singh. For many years now, the chiropractic industry has claimed to be able to cure all kinds of illnesses, such as ear infections and asthma. Mr Singh _____ᶜ when he wrote an opinion piece in the *Sunday Times*. The British Chiropractors' Association immediately took him to court, where he lost the case. The judge argued that Mr Singh was claiming facts he could not prove.

By the time the Court of Appeal reversed the decision, Mr Singh had a legal bill of £200,000. Fortunately for Mr Singh, he was a successful author and could afford to fight. However, _____ᵈ in similar cases involving the less wealthy, scientists might not be able to afford such costs to defend themselves. _____ᵉ libel laws may well put unwelcome restrictions on scientists' rights to express opinions on matters of public interest.

# Understanding written information

**By the end of Part B you will be able to:**

- identify key vocabulary
- use prepositional phrases
- express possibility.

## 1 Identifying key vocabulary

> When you find unknown or new words in a written text, try to understand the general ideas in the text before you start looking in your dictionary.

**1a** Work in pairs. Ask and answer these questions.

  **1** Do you know what geo-engineering is?

  **2** Do you know of any examples of geo-engineering?

**1b** Read the text below. Answer these questions in your own words.

  **1** What are the aims of geo-engineering?

  **2** Why do researchers feel this science is necessary?

  **3** What methods do geo-engineers suggest to achieve their aims?

### Geo-engineering

Geo-engineering is a new branch of science, concerned with reducing the effects of global warming. It is based on the theory that cutting the emissions of carbon dioxide into the atmosphere will not happen fast enough to delay the harmful consequences of rising temperatures over the next century. Therefore, mankind should experiment with large-scale engineering projects which would help to cool the planet.

**1c** Check your answers with a partner.

**1d** Match the extracts (A–D) on p.113 giving examples of geo-engineering with the summaries (1–4). Do not worry about understanding all the words. Try to understand the main idea.

**A**

One proposal is a giant floating umbrella, which would act like a blanket of cloud to shade parts of the earth from the sun. A similar idea would be to inject sulphate particles into the stratosphere to cool the sun's rays, or the creation of clouds artificially by spraying seawater into the atmosphere.

**B**

A scheme to pour iron into the sea in order to encourage the growth of carbon-eating plankton (a tiny sea creature) was stopped after fears were raised that, if successful, this might consume all the oxygen in those parts of the ocean and thereby kill all other sea creatures.

**C**

Some scientists are now claiming that a more direct way to reduce $CO_2$ levels is to set up industrial plants which collect the gas from the air. Small-scale versions of these machines already operate on board submarines, where they prevent $CO_2$ concentrations from reaching dangerous levels.

**D**

The light bulb we have been using for over a hundred years is highly inefficient, since only five per cent of the energy used is turned into light, the rest being lost as heat. Additionally, it only has a life of about 1,000 hours. As a result many countries are now replacing these with more energy-efficient compact fluorescent lights.

**1** The use of machines that remove and store carbon dioxide

**2** The creation of an object in the sky to prevent the sun from reaching the earth

**3** Changes to an everyday object in people's homes

**4** Changing a natural habitat

**1e** Underline important or 'key' words in the texts which helped you to match the summary with the text. Compare your answers in pairs.

**1f** Answer these questions about the texts.

**Text A** How many different inventions are mentioned to prevent the sun reaching the earth?

**Text B** Why was this scheme stopped?

**Text C** Where is this technology already commonly in use?

**Text D** Why does the traditional light bulb need to be replaced?

**1g** Underline any words you will need to understand in order to use the ideas of these texts in an essay or a presentation.

## 2 Using prepositional phrases

> Prepositional phrases begin with a preposition (*in*, *with*, *from*, etc.) and end with a noun.
>
> ***Example***
>
> *… from the air.*
>
> Prepositional phrases are often used after verbs or nouns to give more information about place, direction, time or type.
>
> ***Examples***
>
> *… for a hundred years … – time*
>
> *… many countries in the world … – place*
>
> *… to pour iron into the sea … – direction*
>
> *… replacing these with more energy-efficient lights … – type*

**2a** Look at the underlined prepositional phrases in the text below. Does the prepositional phrase give information about time, place, type or direction? Write your answers in the table.

> Geo-engineering is a new branch of science, concerned with reducing the effects of global warming[1]. It is based on the theory[2] that cutting the emissions of carbon dioxide[3] into the atmosphere[4] will not happen fast enough to delay the harmful consequences of rising temperatures[5] in the world[6] over the next century[7].

| Function of prepositional phrase | Examples |
|---|---|
| To give information about place | |
| To give information about time | |
| To give information about direction | |
| To give information about type (of something) | |

> Prepositions also commonly follow certain words.
>
> ***Examples***
>
> *think **about** something (verb + preposition)*
>
> *be aware **of** something (adjective + preposition)*
>
> *a solution **to** something (noun + preposition)*

**2b** Look at this dictionary entry for *concerned*. Use it to complete sentences 1–3 with a suitable preposition.

> **concerned (adj) 1** ~ (about/with sth) interested in something *Scientists are concerned with reducing $CO_2$ emissions.*
>
> **2** ~ (about/for sth) | ~ (that) worried *They are concerned about the effects of the experiment. I was concerned for my sister's health.*

1 It was getting dark and the research team was concerned _____ finishing the project on time.

2 Much of the first part of the text was concerned _____ the possible negative effects.

3 The research team was concerned _____ the other creatures in the sea.

**2c** Complete these sentences with the correct preposition. Use a dictionary to help you.

**1 effect** (n)
   a The change in temperature had absolutely no effect _____ the results.
   b Many people felt the effects _____ the volcano for several days.

**2 rise** (v & n)
   a The number of people suffering from the disease fell in 2010, but there was a rise _____ 50% the following year.
   b The number of people who applied for the course rose _____ 50% in the following year to 780.
   c There was a significant rise _____ the number of staff in 2009.

**3 benefit** (v & n)
   a The local people are unlikely to benefit _____ the construction of the hotel.
   b The second proposal has the benefit _____ costing less.
   c A decrease in global temperatures will be of benefit _____ those living in the poorest areas.

**4 question** (v & n)
   a There is no question _____ the project being delayed.
   b The researchers were asked some difficult questions _____ safety and affordability.

## 3  Expressing possibility

**3a** Work in pairs. Look at these scientific predictions made by the writer Raymond Kurzweil. Discuss which you think are more likely to occur in the next twenty years.

1 Telephones will be able to translate between languages as you speak.

2 Intelligent 'exoskeletal' legs will be attached around the outside of limbs, and will allow people who currently use wheelchairs to walk.

3 Robots will replace humans as the drivers of vehicles.

4 Computers will be miniaturized and will be found embedded everywhere, including in jewellery, walls and clothing.

**3b** Read this extract from a student essay about the role of technology in the future. Which predictions from your discussion in 3a are mentioned in the extract?

> Another influence on the possible direction of technology in the future is environmental factors. The world is finite and has finite resources. In all areas of technology, resources and power are needed to produce the parts and components to make it work, and this means that future technological development is highly likely to be limited to what is physically possible. I will illustrate this with some well-known technological predictions put forward by Kurzweil (1990). Firstly, he predicted that robots will drive vehicles instead of humans by using wireless communication between their own vehicle and sensors placed along the roads and in other cars. According to Brewster (2009), there is a strong possibility that the world will have used up its oil and metal resources by 2200, so it is therefore unlikely that metal or plastic (oil-based) vehicles will exist. Secondly, he predicted that miniaturized computers will be found 'embedded everywhere' (Kurzweil, 1990). Admittedly, the computers may be much smaller than present ones, but it is very probable that the numbers predicted could use vast amounts of valuable and costly raw materials. Finally, he suggested the idea that telephones will be able to translate between languages as people speak. This is an attractive idea, but the resources needed to maintain, even potentially increase, present phone ownership levels and provide all the transmission centres needed, are again extremely large. Add to this the environmental problems of disposing of all the old phones as new models become available, and there is a chance that phones might not even exist fifty years from now.

**3c** Check your answers with a partner. Discuss whether you agree with Raymond Kurzweil's arguments.

**3d** Underline any words or phrases used to express probability in the extract in 3b. Write the words and phrases in the table below.

| Language of possibility | Examples |
| --- | --- |
| Modals | *could* |
| Adjectives | *possible* |
| Nouns | *likelihood* |

**3e** Using the ideas in 3b and the words and phrases from 3d, write five sentences about future predictions.

*Example*

*Computers <u>could</u> be embedded in our bodies.*

1 _____

2 _____

3 _____

4 _____

5 _____

**3f** Complete this extract from a student's essay using words and phrases from the table in 3d. There may be more than one possible answer.

> One area where technology <u>may</u> play a major role is in solving the problems of global warming. With the strong _____[1] that world temperatures will increase further and the consequent _____[2] effects of rises in sea level, it_____[3] be that technology offers the best way out. One _____[4] idea (Flood & Price, 2009) is to inject sulphate particles into the atmosphere to reflect the sun's rays back into space. However, it is uncertain if this would be successful for a number of reasons. Firstly, there is a distinct _____[5] that this would account for only less than 50 per cent of the warming; and secondly, the _____[6] of environmental pollution would be quite high.

**3g** Compare your answers with a partner.

**3h** Work in pairs. Decide whether you think these predictions are highly likely (HL), possible (P) or unlikely (U). Explain your reasons.

  1 Most countries will replace traditional light bulbs with more energy-efficient compact fluorescent lights. _____

  2 Most learning will be done at home using software or 'computer teachers'. _____

  3 There will be a world government by the year 2020. _____

  4 People with impaired vision will wear special 'glasses' that will speak to them and tell them what their surroundings are like. _____

  5 Clothes will be developed to control the temperature around the body, so that people are never too cold or too hot. _____

**3i** Rewrite the sentences in 3h using words and phrases from the table in 3d to reflect how likely you think they are.

**3j** Work in pairs. Discuss the likelihood of these situations. Try to use expressions of possibility.

  1 People will be able to upload their minds onto a computer.

  2 People will be able to communicate with computers by two-way speech, not through the keyboard.

  3 Personal flying vehicles will be commonplace.

  4 Classrooms will be dominated by computers with intelligent courseware, tailored to individual ability and personality.

  5 Working from home via computer will become much more common.

  6 Phone calls will be made using three-dimensional holographic images.

## Hedging

As we saw in Unit 2, academic writing tends to be cautious. Researchers are very aware that what we know today is only a partial truth, and that much of what we learn today will be modified or may even be completely disproven at some time in the future. Compare these two sentences.

*GM foods __are__ dangerous, as some research concluded that there are long-term risks.*

*GM foods __may be__ dangerous, but long-term research in this field is unavailable.*

The first sentence is too confident for an academic context; the second is more cautious because it accepts that we do not know the definite answer to this question. We often refer to the language used to express caution as *hedging*. Common examples of hedging are:

*The research **suggests** that ...*

*There **seems to** be a link between ...*

*There **may** be concerns about future developments ...*

*It **appears that** ...*

*There **may well** be ...*

**3k** Look at these extracts from a student's essay examining the possible outcomes of using the geo-engineering ideas in 1d. Rewrite the sentences using hedging language to make them more cautious.

*Example*
*The cloud will change the weather patterns.*
*There may well be a change in weather patterns if the cloud is introduced.*

**1** The umbrella will use too much $CO_2$ in the building process.

_____

**2** The project to encourage sea life will create problems with international law.

_____

**3** Building $CO_2$ storage plants will be too expensive.

_____

**4** There will be problems with releasing the $CO_2$ back into the atmosphere.

_____

> **LESSON TASK**  **4 Reading critically**

**4a** Skim the texts on pp.119 and 120. What topic are they about?

**4b** Scan the texts and underline any key topic vocabulary. Check the words and phrases in a dictionary if necessary.

# An expensive hobby

Jack Brown examines the arguments against the Space Industry.

The Space Industry has attracted criticism since its very earliest days. With the loss of the $165million Mars Polar Lander and the $125million Mars Climate Orbiter within two years of each other, many Americans seriously questioned whether NASA should receive as much tax-payer funding as they do. In fact, NASA has been facing the same kind of losses and similar challenges to its funding programme for the last 40 years.

Many supporters of space research have tried to argue that the projects justify their expense because of the results that they achieve. Yet over 95% of the oceans of our own planet remain unexplored, and there is evidence to suggest that these may provide just as many breakthroughs in the area of science as space at a much cheaper cost to the tax payer.

The majority of research breakthroughs occur in ground-based studies, rather than in research actually carried out in space. Given that NASA spends over a third of its budget maintaining the International Space Station and the Shuttle links between Earth and the station, the few discoveries that have come from manned space flights fail to justify the excessive amounts spent on them.

As most space agencies are so closely linked to the military in their countries, any spin-off benefits from space exploration usually benefit the military, not the general public.

It is clear that with 60% of the US population opposed to the funding of space research through taxes, there is little justification to keep dipping into the public purse. The success of the $10 million X Prize, in which individuals were invited to compete to design an effective space vehicle, has proven that space projects can be successfully funded privately. And over 11,000 people have already signed up for Virgin's 'Galactica' private space experience.

Although the arguments in favour of space funding appear attractive, in real terms people benefit very little from their investment.

**2**

## Mankind's best safety net

It is in the nature of man to be curious. Without the desire to discover, our world would be without many of the inventions that make modern life more comfortable. Space exploration is a natural extension of that.

Although the $15.5 billion budget that NASA presented to the American public in 2006 seems huge, it only represents a tiny percentage of total government spending. To put it into perspective, the American public chose to spend a whopping $31 billion on their pets, twice as much as the space budget. In fact, if the government stopped investing in space research, the poor person on the street would have $1.03 in their pocket, rather than $1. It's not really enough to be noticed.

However, the benefits in return for that 3 cents are huge. NASA has a responsibility to bring its astronauts back alive and well, which means that medical and safety equipment must be absolutely fail-safe. The standards that space equipment are tested against are far greater than anything the car industry, for example, tests against.

This technology can be passed down to the general public in safer systems. The air industry benefits from higher standards of aerodynamics thanks to research at NASA. Even our cooking benefits – Teflon, the material that coats non-stick saucepans, was a NASA invention.

If that weren't enough, the space industry stimulates the economy. Even in Britain, a country not known for its space research, over 60,000 are directly employed in the aerospace industry, and at least twice as many again depend on the industry indirectly.

The strongest argument in favour of current space research comes down to simple risk strategy. Relying solely on planet Earth for the future existence of the human race is a risky strategy. The chances of an asteroid collision are significantly high enough to cause concern among those in the field. There is a real probability that if Mars contains ice, it contains the fundamental elements of life, and more importantly the potential to sustain a climate humans could live in. It makes sense to have an escape route planned.

**4c**  You have been asked to consider this question:

*Can the public funding of space exploration be justified?*

Work in pairs. Each read one of the articles about space exploration in detail. As you read, write notes on the possible consequences of ending public funding of space research. Add anything you already know that supports the arguments to your notes.

**4d**  Work in pairs. Share and compare information from the two texts, referring only to your notes. Try to express your ideas using a range of expressions. Are there any relevant points that you think the texts have missed?

## 5  Review and extension

### Prepositional phrases

**5a**  Look at the extracts on p.121 from a student discussion about problems with reading in English for academic study. Identify and underline the prepositional phrases.

I had to do a huge amount of reading, but I just couldn't cope with it all in the beginning. After a while, I asked some friends for advice about my problems and they suggested I make a timetable of work for reading the titles I had been given.

*Shayan, 24, Iran*

I had a problem with understanding what I needed to read. I thought I had to understand every word on the page! If I didn't, I'd start worrying about things. Because I was trying hard to understand everything, I ended up understanding nothing. Finally, someone else on my course recommended just reading for the main idea. These days I try to do that, and I make a note of any key vocabulary and then write it in my notebook after I've finished.

*Fei Fei, 22, China*

**5b** Complete the underlined prepositional phrases in this text by using suitable prepositions (there may be more than one answer).

A hotel _____ China[1] has a unique receptionist working _____ the front desk.[2] Although she speaks and receives guests _____ the usual polite phrases[3], she is non-human. Although the use _____ robots to replace humans[4] leaves most people feeling highly uncomfortable, robots are increasingly being used _____ a number[5] of different situations.

The International Federation of Robotics estimated that _____ 2008[6], over a million robots were being used _____ the world[7]. However, _____ many people[8], the image _____ robots[9] is linked _____ science fiction writing and films[10]. _____ those films[11], robots are often shown as a threat to our existence and often seen _____ inhuman[12], _____ a complete lack[13] of emotion and moral values.

These are concerns that the robotics industry will have to address if they want the general public to welcome robots _____ their everyday lives[14].

## Expressing possibility

**5c** Five of these sentences contain an error using the language of probability. Find and correct the errors, or mark the correct sentences with a tick (✓).

***Examples***    *that new drugs will be created*
*It is highly likely* ~~*to create new drugs*~~ *from genetic testing in the future.*

---

*There is a strong probability that it will work.*         ✓

**1** There is a little chance that the system will be affordable for the foreseeable future.

---

**2** The probability to spend less on research in the future is low.

---

**3** There is a strong chance that the project will provide long-term benefits.

---

**4** It is considerably unlikely that all domestic work will be done by robots in the near future.

---

**5** The Hedron project is likely that it will produce fascinating results.

---

**6** The likelihood of environmental damage is too high.

---

**7** The change in the law is probable to cause confusion at first.

---

**8** The researchers failed to mention likely side effects.

---

**5d** Look at the notes a student has made while reading a text on genetics, and write complete sentences. Use hedging language.

***Example***
*Human personality = influenced / genes*
*It appears that human personality is influenced by genes.*

**1** Environment = play / important part in / human personality

---

**2** Research / relationship between / two = more complicated than we think

---

**3** Genes = main influence in things, e.g. height

---

**4** One study / taller people = experience advantages in / workplace

---

**5** This = genes = affect things, e.g. income

---

# Investigating

**By the end of Part C you will be able to:**
- recognize your reading level
- use synonyms
- understand substitution.

## 1 Recognizing your reading level

> When you are researching a new topic, you will find some texts more difficult to understand than others. This is because texts vary in their complexity. It is important that you know which level you are currently at, and to work towards a higher level of reading comprehension.

**1a** Work in pairs. You are going to read three extracts from articles about animal testing in science taken from a medical journal.

    **1** Create a mind map of words you expect to appear in the texts.

    **2** Brainstorm the arguments you already know either in favour of or against animal testing.

**1b** Scan the texts for the words in your mind map.

**A**

Animal testing, also known as animal experimentation, or animal research, is the use of animals in the fields of medicine, behavioural sciences, military defence and the cosmetic industry. This research is strictly regulated in the United Kingdom. Internationally, animal testing differs depending on the institution and the animal species. Organizations in favour of animal testing argue that without it, few of the advances in medical care in the last century would have been possible. They argue that even modern computer programs are unable to predict how the body will behave. Organizations which are against the testing of animals claim that this practice provides unreliable information and is unnecessarily cruel to the animals.

It is difficult to estimate the scale of animal testing, but sources suggest that approximately 100 million non-human mammals are tested on annually. The majority, approximately three-quarters of all the animals involved, are mice, rats or other rodents.

**B**

Many people overlook the role that animal research has played in their own lives. Medical research is a long, drawn-out process, and by the time most therapies, vaccinations and treatments reach the patient, they have forgotten the many stages that led to that drug being accepted. Not least of these is the process of animal testing. Scientists have worked hard to develop alternatives to animal testing, such as computer modelling programs, but there are some areas where more information is needed. Animal testing has proved successful in developing flu vaccinations, and perfecting surgical techniques. They are now working on some of the bigger medical challenges, such as cures for HIV, cancer and brain damage, such as that caused by Alzheimer's.

The longer, healthier lives that we now enjoy are largely thanks to a better understanding of how the body works, which has been advanced through this type of research. And humans are not the only ones to benefit, as the advances made are used in veterinary, as well as medical, science.

Thanks to legislation, the living standards of animals being kept for testing has improved, and there is now greater awareness of the need to communicate information between professionals, to ensure that no research will be unnecessarily duplicated by scientists around the world.

**C**

Testing on animals is indefensible both morally and scientifically. Although legislation exists in the United States to ensure that animals in the care of scientific researchers are treated humanely, such legislation excludes the care of birds, rodents and other small animals, which make up the majority of the animals currently being studied. This means that huge numbers of animals have no legal protection from cruelty at all. Not only this, but the use of different species in the testing of drugs provides unreliable data, and this in turn can have a negative effect when the drug is later tested on human patients.

An additional weakness in the current legislation is that it prioritizes research goals over any other aims. Therefore, the care of any creatures involved in experimentation is secondary to ensuring that medical objectives are achieved. Such practices justify any number of cruelties. Given that many countries are aggressively competing in the pharmaceutical field for the lucrative profits that inevitably come with the development of an effective new drug, it stands to reason that the amount of research conducted will inevitably rise, as will the number of animals suffering unnecessarily in the name of drug company profits and shareholders.

**1c** Match the headings (1–4) with the texts (A–C). There is one heading you will not need.

**1** An overview of key issues in animal testing

**2** Recent changes to the law on animal testing

**3** Animal research as a benefit to all species

**4** Animal research is unjustified

**1d** Read the texts again and answer these questions. Choose the correct option (a–c).

**Text A**

**1** What argument do people who support animal experiments use to justify their views?
  **a** the progress made in the field of behavioural sciences
  **b** the historical success of healthcare developments
  **c** the use of computer programs to support the results of animal testing

**2** What is known about the animals used in tests?
  **a** Rats and mice make better subjects than other animals.
  **b** There are few larger animals used in animal testing.
  **c** Around 75 million rodents are used in animal research each year.

**Text B**

3 The author argues that many people fail to appreciate animal testing because
  **a** there is a large time lapse between testing and receiving treatment.
  **b** they have not directly benefited from the advancements.
  **c** the tests often involve more than one type of experiment.

4 According to the author, in the future animal testing will benefit from
  **a** the application of the findings in treating animals.
  **b** the development of new laws to guarantee better standards.
  **c** the introduction of better means of sharing results among the scientific community.

**Text C**

5 The author states that many animals suffer unnecessarily because
  **a** researchers experimenting on animals lack ethical values.
  **b** researchers select animals that do not react in the same way as humans.
  **c** the law does not offer protection for certain species.

6 The author anticipates an increase in the number of animal experiments due to
  **a** intense commercial competition.
  **b** the appeal of animal testing among those who finance the research.
  **c** the lack of objection to the process of animal testing.

**1e** Work in pairs. Discuss these questions.

1 Which questions did you find easiest to answer? Why?

2 Which questions did you find most challenging? Why?

3 Can you identify any of the features that make the text easier or more difficult?

> All three texts contain some topic-specific vocabulary, making them challenging for intermediate-level students. As the texts become more difficult, the language used, the sentence structure and the use of substitution (replacing one word with another) become more varied. The level of ideas also becomes increasingly complex.
>
> When you are selecting a text for your research, one of the factors you need to consider is its level of difficulty. Some texts that are relevant to the topic may simply be above your current level of understanding. However, if a text is well below your level of understanding, the ideas it covers may be limited to describing concepts and giving definitions, which is useful, but an over-reliance on these kinds of texts is not encouraged. Although it is best to use the full range of texts, you may need to build up gradually to using high-level texts.

## 2  Using synonyms

> Synonyms (words with a similar meaning) are very useful in academic work. They can help you avoid plagiarism when you paraphrase other writers' ideas and they give variety to your academic writing. They can also be useful when you search for source texts.

**2a** You are going to read an extract from an academic text book about the social effects of changes in technology in the first half of the 20th century. Before you read, decide whether the groups of words on p.126 are adjectives, nouns or verbs.

| 1 _____ | | 2 _____ | | 3 _____ | |
| --- | --- | --- | --- | --- | --- |
| creation | _____ | caused | _____ | important | *striking* |
| dullness | _____ | claimed | _____ | opposite | _____ |
| features | *aspects* | presented | _____ | uncommon | _____ |
| machines | _____ | stimulated | _____ | unwilling | _____ |
| opinion | _____ | | | | |
| tendency | _____ | | | | |
| time | _____ | | | | |

**2b** Read the extract. Match the words in bold with their synonyms in 2a.

One of the most **striking aspects** of the post-war period was the disappearance of servants from many middle-class homes. Maids and cooks became **scarce**, and when they were still found they could expect higher wages. It has been **argued** (Hare, 2001) that this **trend** was **provoked** by the spread of household electrical equipment, such as the vacuum cleaner and the cooker. Certainly, this was the **period** when many urban areas were connected to mains electricity, making possible the use of these labour-saving **devices**. However, a **contrary view** is **put forward** by Gilbert and Leaviss (1998), who claim that the **development** of such machines was **encouraged** by the lack of servants, rather than the other way round. It seems that many women who had found independence in factory work during the First World War were **reluctant** to return to the **monotony** of domestic work afterwards, and this stimulated the production of the irons, toasters and fridges, which were soon to become common in homes.

A useful source of synonyms is a *thesaurus*. Many word processing programs have a thesaurus built in, and there are a number of different ones available free online. Also, some learner dictionaries may have synonyms for words.

A typical thesaurus entry will give a number of different synonyms for a word, grouped by different word class and meaning of the word.

*Example*

*common (adjective):*

1 *ordinary* widespread, frequent, general, universal, familiar, regular, rare (antonym).

2 *everyday* usual, customary, familiar, normal, nothing special, ordinary, conventional, unexceptional, regular, extraordinary (antonym).

3 *shared* mutual, joint, public, for all, communal, collective, private (antonym).

4 *vulgar* coarse, ill-mannered, rough, low-class, unrefined, refined (antonym).

*common (noun):*

*green* park, open space, playing field, playground, recreational area

To choose a suitable synonym, you need to know what type of word it is (e.g. noun, adjective, verb) and understand its meaning in the context you find it. A dictionary will give you further information about the meaning and use of synonyms.

**2c** Work in pairs. Read this extract and discuss these questions.

> It seems that many women who had found independence in factory work during the First World War were reluctant to return to the monotony of domestic work afterwards, and this stimulated the production of the irons, toasters and fridges, which were soon to become **common**.

1 Is *common* used as a noun or an adjective in this extract?
2 Which group(s) of words in the example thesaurus entry on p.126 are the most similar in meaning to the way 'common' is used in this extract?
3 Which two or three words do you think would be the most suitable synonyms?

**2d** Match the words in bold in this extract from the same text book with the thesaurus entries below. Then choose a suitable synonym for each word using the questions in 2c to help you.

> During the period after the war, in fact, a **breakdown** in the social class **system** in the UK was becoming increasingly **evident**. How much this was due to technological change, and how far these social changes **affected** the rate and **extent** of technological innovation, may be difficult to **evaluate**.

1 Word in extract: *extent*
  **degree (n.)** amount, level, scope
  **size (n.)** area, limit, boundary

2 Word in extract: _____
  **obvious (adj.)** plain, apparent, clear, unmistakable

3 Word in extract: _____
  **stop working (v.)** fail, collapse, go down
  **divide (v.)** classify, categorize, group, separate
  **analysis (n.)** itemization, classification, categorization, analysis
  **failure (n.)** collapse, halt, interruption

4 Word in extract: _____
  **assess (v.)** appraise, weigh up, estimate, calculate

5 Word in extract: _____
  **order (n.)** organization, arrangement, classification, structure
  **method (n.)** technique, procedure, approach, routine
  **orderliness (n.)** regularity, logic

6 Word in extract: _____
  **distress (v.)** touch, disturb, upset
  **have an effect on (v.)** influence, shape, involve, change
  **assume (v.)** pretend to have, imitate

> When recording new words in your vocabulary logbooks, it is helpful to also record one or two common synonyms for each meaning which you can use when paraphrasing.

**2e** Complete these sentences (1–7) with the most suitable word from each pair of synonyms. Then choose a reason why the other synonym is unsuitable in each sentence.

> wrong collocation      wrong grammar      wrong meaning      wrong preposition
> wrong register (formal/informal)      wrong word form

### Example
**contrast / differ**

*The results from the team at MIT <u>differ</u> from those at Reading University in several ways.*

*Wrong preposition: contrast* **with**

**1 characteristics / components**

The _____ of the brain are so varied it is unlikely that we will ever be able to duplicate it through technology.

**2 interrogated / questioned**

Experts have _____ the argument that all animal testing is justified.

**3 all over the place / widespread**

The use of chemicals in farming is _____ in many countries.

**4 finance / investment**

The government has agreed to _____ the research project for the next ten years.

**5 adapt / modify**

Many animals simply fail to _____ to the changes in their environment.

**6 answer / react**

The chemicals _____ differently in extreme temperatures.

**7 implications / ramifications**

The results of the new study have very positive _____ for people working in the field.

## 3   Understanding substitution

> Often a text will avoid repetition of words by using forms of substitution, such as pronouns.
>
> Common pronouns are *it, they, this, these, that, those, such, so* and *one*.
>
> ### Examples
>
> ***Maids and cooks** became scarce, and when **they** were still found **they** could expect higher wages.*
>
> *During the period after the war, **a breakdown in the social class system** in the UK was becoming increasingly evident. How much **this** was due to technological change …*

**3a** Look at these extracts from the texts in 1b. Identify which previously mentioned word or phrase the words in bold refer back to. Write your answers in the table on p.129.

1 Animal testing, also known as animal experimentation, or animal research, is the use of animals in the fields of medicine, behavioural sciences, military defence and the cosmetics industry. **This research** is strictly regulated in the United Kingdom.

2 Organizations in favour of animal testing argue that without **it**, few of the advances in medical care in the last century would have been possible. **They** argue that even modern computer programs are unable to predict how the body will behave.

3 Organizations which are against the testing of animals claim that **this practice** provides unreliable information and is unnecessarily cruel to the animals.

4 Many people overlook the role that animal research has played in **their** own lives.

5 Although legislation exists in the United States to ensure that animals in the care of scientific researchers are treated humanely, **such legislation** excludes the care of birds, rodents and other small animals …

| Back reference | What it refers to |
|---|---|
| *Example* | |
| **1** *This research* | *Animal testing / animal research* |
| **2** *it* | |
| **3** *they* | |
| **4** *this practice* | |
| **5** *their* | |
| **6** *such legislation* | |

**3b** Underline the words which refer back in sentences 1–8 below and draw an arrow ( ← ) to the word or phrase substituted.

*Example*

*The statistics from 2010 were considerably higher than <u>those</u> from 2000.*

1 Mammals evolved millions of years ago. At that time, the only threat to plants was birds and disease.

2 Animal testing is a controversial issue. Groups who oppose it often do so quite verbally.

3 The survey targeted the 16–24 age group. Those who were approached tended to be either in higher education or intending to study later.

4 There has been a general improvement in girls' exam results in science and technology. It has been suggested that this change may be the result of new teaching methods.

5 Scientists have been concerned about the effects of long periods of time in space. These might include both physical and psychological reactions.

6 Establishing a research centre at the Antarctic is always problematic. Such a task often needs the financial backing of a large group of companies.

7 There are many effects of global warming. The one which concerns most people who work in this area is rising sea levels.

8 There have been many technical innovations in the field of mobile phone technology. Such developments are often driven by commercial needs, rather than science.

> **LESSON TASK**    4 Following academic sources

You and a partner are going to give a short presentation (five minutes) on the question: 'Does the current legislation in the UK regarding animal testing need to be tightened further?'

**4a** Work in pairs. Read the extract below from a student dissertation and answer these questions.

1 What is the name of the law which controls the testing of animals in the UK?

2 When was the law introduced?

3 What are the three areas for which the researchers must obtain licences?

4 What must the head researcher prove?

5 What must the agency prove?

6 Who has overall responsibility for the care of the animals?

The Animals Act, which is also known as the Scientific Procedures Act, was introduced in the UK in 1986. This law regulates the use of animals in scientific testing. There were a number of negative cases appearing in the press where animals were clearly mistreated in the UK around this time, and it was felt that any such research needed to be governed by three different licences before experimentation could take place. The first of these is a project licence, which is granted to the head researcher who oversees the experiments. This licence sets out the number of animals and the species to be used in the experiment. The nature of the tests themselves and the objectives of the research are also specified before this licence can be given. To be granted a licence, the head researcher needs to be able to demonstrate that the potential negative effect on the animal is outweighed by the potential benefits of the research. Any projects that fail to meet these requirements will be turned down. In addition, if it is possible, researchers should only use animals with a known low sensitivity to pain. If it is impossible to do so, pain should be minimized through the use of anaesthetics and pain relievers.

The second licence involves certification for the agency, in other words those who are responsible for conducting the tests. Agencies are required to provide the space, staffing and facilities to handle the experiment to the required standard. Only when they do so will they be given the licence. The final licence is individual and is granted to the researcher or technician who will directly carry out the experiment. These individuals are legally responsible for the welfare of the animals. The law was designed to ensure that those who carry out tests on animals are accountable for their actions, and that any such research is transparent.

**4b** Work in pairs. Underline the words that substitute something that has been mentioned before. Discuss which words or phrases these refer back to.

**4c** Work in pairs. Prepare a five-minute presentation on the question 'Does the current legislation in the UK regarding animal testing need to be tightened further?'

1 Look again at the texts in 1b. What ideas and information would be useful in your presentation?

2 What order are you going to put your ideas in?

3 Make a list of possible synonyms or re-phrases of any key words.

4 Check that your conclusions reflect the content of your research.

**4d** Work in groups. Take turns to give your pair presentation.

## 5 Review and extension

### Substitution

**5a** Complete the extract below from an applied science text book using the referencing words in the list. You can use any word more than once and you will not need all of the words.

| one | that | these | this | those |
|-----|------|-------|------|-------|

One of the more modern developments in science is *that* of Molecular Gastronomy. Prof. Nicholas Kurti was a nuclear scientist, working in the field of nuclear cooling. _____[1] was a field which was traditionally applied to technical developments in heavy industry, but Kurti had a passion for cooking. He was interested in the contribution science had made to society through the development of cooking processes and was keen to see if _____[2] progress could be taken even further to develop new dishes. To do _____[3], he needed the help of other physicists and professionals from the catering industry. The organization he founded had several objectives, only _____[4] of which remains today – to understand the technical components of cooking. _____[5] is achieved through the development of understanding of aroma, texture and flavour. _____[6] tended to interact with each other, and various cooking methods could transform our perception of them. He was able to prove various theories wrong, such as the necessity of adding salt to the cooking water of green vegetables or searing meat (cooking it briefly at a high temperature) to seal in the juices. _____[7] developments have been enthusiastically adopted by _____[8] who work at the top end of the catering industry today.

**5b** Read this extract from an academic text book on climate change. Decide whether each word in bold is a noun, adjective or verb. Write N, A or V in the second column in the table on p.132.

One **proposal** for preventing the sun from overheating the earth's atmosphere is to build a **giant** parasol, which would act like a blanket of cloud to shade parts of the earth from the sun. In recent **research**, Lenton and Vaughan (2009) tried to analyze and evaluate the likely **effectiveness** of such a project, without regard to cost. They found that the solar umbrella would have to be half the size of Brazil (four million square kilometres) merely in order to **counterbalance** half the **expected** warming over the next century. Clearly, **building** and **maintaining** such a **structure** would be an immensely challenging task.

| Original word | Type of word (in context) | Synonyms |
|---|---|---|
| proposal | N | plan, scheme |
| giant | | |
| research | | |
| effectiveness | | |
| counterbalance | | |
| expected | | |
| building | | |
| maintaining | | |
| structure | | |

**5c** Write two synonyms for each of the words in the table in 5b that you could use to paraphrase. Use a thesaurus to help you.

**5d** Match the pairs of sentences (1–8) and (a–h).

**1** There has been considerable interest in the development of nuclear science among an unlikely group – environmentalists.

**a** One which has gained considerable attention is the possibility of creating replacement body parts in the future.

**2** There is a need for scientists to engage with the public more through media management.

**b** Such forms of assessment provide results that are of little use to either universities or industry.

**3** The UK predicts that the gaming industry will become one of the fastest-growing sectors of the UK economy in the next ten years.

**c** While these people were opposed to this energy technology in the past, on the grounds that it produced hazardous waste, they have now come round to the possible benefits.

**4** There are many applications of research into successfully creating and implanting artificial DNA.

**d** The loss of such a store of DNA would be tragic and only too possible if global warming and deforestation continue.

**5** Many of the world's rainforests contain a wealth of genetic information.

**e** A good example of this is Australia, which has taken the majority of titles in this field in recent years.

**6** School science exams have been criticized recently for testing memory skills rather than deeper knowledge.

**f** Research has suggested that those who are more directly affected by issues are often more willing to take action.

**7** Many successful environmental projects are often carried out at a grass-roots level, among local communities.

**g** This growth is partly the result of the pool of talent in this field, and also government funding in this area.

**8** The application of science in sports has given many countries an advantage in international competitions, such as the Olympic Games.

**h** It seems that those researchers who do so tend to find that their work is more positively received.

# Reporting in speech

**By the end of Part D you will be able to:**

- use signpost words and phrases in presentations
- deal with questions
- use intonation to maintain interest
- refer to visual materials.

## 1   Using signpost words and phrases in presentations

> You have already looked at the importance of signpost phrases in helping you to follow a lecture in Part A of this unit. In this Part, you will look at how to use those signpost phrases to make your own presentations more effective.

**1a**  Work in pairs. Think about two talks you have listened to, either in English or in another language. Answer these questions.

**1** How did the speaker get the audience's interest at the start of their talk?

**2** Did the audience choose to be there?

**3** How did the audience know when the talk had come to an end?

**4** Did the audience ask any questions? When?

**5** Which talk was better? Why?

**Introductions and conclusions**

**1b**  Read these extracts from two different presentations. Match each extract (a–g) with the correct presentation and stage in the presentation in the table on p.134.

**a** However, in the final analysis, due to the inherent unreliability of the weather, we may still need to depend on other sources of power to provide our energy.

**b** One of the world's most pressing issues is waste disposal.

**c** The first advantage is that this form of power is clean compared to other energy sources.

**d** Finally, the benefits of this energy source have not yet been proven over the long term.

**e** I'd like to talk today about wind energy.

**f** To sum up, the problem of reducing the amount going to landfills is not one that will go away quickly.

**g** According to a government study, about 29 million tonnes of this were from household waste. The question is: what can we do?

|  | Wind power | Waste disposal |
|---|---|---|
| Introduction / early in the talk |  |  |
| Conclusion / later in the talk | a |  |

**1c** Write the signpost words and phrases from the extracts in 1b.

*Example*
*However, in the final analysis ...*

b _____

c _____

d _____

e _____

f _____

g _____

> In a presentation, you need to use simple, appropriate and precise language. It is important to get the tone and style of language right from the beginning.

**1d** Match the situations (1–3) with the most appropriate introductory phrases (a–c).

**1** A student giving a presentation to about 30 students from a neighbouring university

**a**
Good morning, ladies and gentlemen. I'd like to welcome you all to ...

**2** A student giving a presentation to about 15 classmates

**b**
Hi, everyone. Thanks for coming here today. Well, as you know, we've been looking at ...

**3** A meeting with about 60 guests from local companies, all dressed formally

**c**
Hi! My name's Keisuke and I represent the IT department here at ...

> As a general rule, if you are giving an academic presentation, the functional language (*Hello, thank you for coming, I'd like to move on to ...*) should be fairly conversational, as this is a more audience-friendly approach. However, you should use topic-specific terms and academic vocabulary for content and avoid general or vague terms and slang.

3.10

**1e** Listen to these extracts from students giving seminar presentations to classmates. Complete this table, indicating whether you think the language used in each introduction is appropriate.

|  | Appropriate? | If not, why not? |
|---|---|---|
| *Example* | *No* | *Too informal, uses informal vocabulary – 'amazing' and linkers, 'so, like'* |
| 1 |  |  |
| 2 |  |  |
| 3 |  |  |
| 4 |  |  |
| 5 |  |  |
| 6 |  |  |

**1f** Compare your answers with a partner.

3.11

**1g** Listen and write the sentences in this table.

| Signpost language to use in an introduction | |
|---|---|
| **Function**<br>Greet the audience and introduce yourself | **Example**<br>*Good morning/afternoon. / Hello / Hi everyone, thanks for coming here.*<br>*I've already met most of you, but for those I haven't, my name's ...* |
| Introduce the topic and provide context | *The main reason I'm here today is to talk about ...*<br>**1** _____<br>*The focus of my presentation is ...*<br>**2** _____<br>*Let me start by telling you a little about how this research project got started ...*<br>**3** _____ |
| Show an awareness of time | *Thank you for your time.*<br>**4** _____<br>*This should only last ten minutes.*<br>*I hope to be finished by ...* |
| Show the organization of your presentation | *I've divided my topic into three sections.*<br>**5** _____<br>*First I'd like to discuss ... , and then we'll move on to the main part of my topic, which is ...*<br>**6** _____ |

**1h** Work in pairs. You are going to give the introduction to a presentation. Use the notes below to prepare your presentation on either wind energy or waste disposal.

| Wind power | Waste disposal |
|---|---|
| Introduction | Introduction |
| Part 1: Advantages | Part 1: Problems with waste |
| Part 2: Disadvantages | Part 2: Possible solutions |
| Part 3: Recommendations – wind energy must be used with other renewable energy sources. | Part 3: Recommendations – general need to reduce the social and environmental impact of waste by adopting all these solutions. |

**1i** Work with another pair of students. Take turns to give your presentation.

> When a speaker ends their presentation, they often:
> **1** remind the audience of the main points
> **2** remind the audience why the issue is significant
> **3** give the audience an opportunity to ask questions.

**1j** Complete the conclusion of a student's presentation on waste disposal with these phrases (a–d).

**a** If there are any questions, please feel free to ask.

**b** I would like to finish by reminding everyone that

**c** In the light of what we have seen, I suggest that

**d** as I have tried to explain this morning, I think the problem of

Well, _____[1] waste disposal is a threat not only to our environment, but also the social well-being of people whose homes are located near landfill sites. _____[2] the solutions proposed should be used in conjunction with each other; in other words, a combination of a number of different solutions is likely to be most successful. _____[3] the problem of waste disposal is only going to become greater as more and more countries industrialize and adopt consumer lifestyles. This is not what we want for our future. _____[4]

3.12

**1k** Listen and check your answers.

**1l** Complete the table on p.137 with the phrases from 1j.

| Signpost language to use in a conclusion | |
|---|---|
| **Function** | **Example** |
| Remind audience of the main points | *So, as we've seen today ...* |
| | *Well, that brings me to the end of my presentation. I'd just like to remind you of the main points ...* |
| | 1 _____ |
| Make a recommendation | *As a result, I suggest that ...* |
| | *My first recommendation is to ...* |
| | 2 _____ |
| Conclude | *In conclusion, I would like to say that ...* |
| | *My final comments concern ...* |
| | 3 _____ |
| Offer to answer questions | *I'll be here at the front for the next ten minutes and I'd be happy to answer any questions ...* |
| | *Thank you very much for your attention and if there are any suggestions or comments, please do contact me at this email address.* |
| | 4 _____ |

**1m** Work in pairs. Write notes for a brief conclusion to the presentation you introduced in 1i using the signpost language in 1l. Take it in turns to present your conclusion.

## 2 Dealing with questions

> Students are encouraged to ask questions at the end of presentations if they are unclear about any of the content or would like more information.
>
> There are three main types of question that are asked at the end of a presentation:
>
> **a** Questions to check a part of the talk which was unclear
>
> **b** Questions to ask for more information
>
> **c** Questions which challenge what the speaker said.

**2a** Match the questions (1–6) with the question types (a–c) above.

**1**
Surely recycling only encourages people to be wasteful? We should be telling them to use less.

**2**
You said you thought we need to use solutions in conjunction with each other. What exactly does that mean?

1 _c_

2 _____

**3**
You said that wind energy is clean compared to other energy sources. Which sources were you thinking of?

3 ____

**4**
You mentioned that wind energy is an eyesore. Can you explain what that means?

4 ____

**5**
You mentioned that wind power is a very old technology, but you also said that the benefits haven't been proven in the long term. Isn't that a contradiction?

5 ____

**6**
Do you know how much more it would cost to increase the number of waste processing plants here in the UK?

6 ____

### Dealing with difficult questions

**2b** Work in pairs. Discuss your definition of a 'difficult' question.

**2c** Work in small groups. Think of strategies to deal with difficult questions.

**2d** Write three questions for the topic of the presentation in 1i that you think your partner will not know the answer to.

**2e** Work in pairs. Take turns to ask and answer your questions. Use the language in this table to help you deal confidently with challenging questions.

| Language to deal with difficult questions | |
|---|---|
| **Function** | **Example** |
| Explain that you are unsure | *Hmm, that's an interesting question.* <br> *That question's not really in my field of expertise. An engineer/economist, etc. would be able to provide a better answer.* |
| Suggest a place where the information can be found | *I would have to go back and have a look on the Internet to see if there's more information on that.* <br> *I believe that there is a book in the library that deals with this topic.* <br> *Well, I haven't got time to go into all the details here, but there's more information on this in ...* |
| Apologize and promise to find out | *I'm afraid I'm going to have to ask my colleagues about that one.* |
| Change the topic | *Well, that's an interesting point, but I think the main issue here is ...* |

## 3 Using intonation to maintain interest

It is essential to use intonation to demonstrate your own interest in a topic, and maintain that of your audience.

3.13

**3a** You will hear sentences about wind energy said in two different ways. Listen and decide which sentence (a or b) is expressed with interest and which is expressed without interest. Complete this table.

| Speaker | ☺ | ☹ |
|---|---|---|
| ***Example*** <br> *I'd like to talk today about wind energy.* | b | a |
| **1** Another advantage is that it's cheap. It may sound obvious, but wind is free. | | |
| **2** Another criticism is that wind energy, by its nature, is intermittent; that is, sometimes the wind blows, sometimes it doesn't. | | |
| **3** According to a government study, about 29 million tonnes of waste was household waste. | | |
| **4** This has a wide range of environmental impacts. Firstly, there is the threat of disease from these sites. | | |
| **5** Moreover, much of what we throw away is non-biodegradable; that is, it does not decompose and will remain in landfill sites for thousands if not millions of years into the future. | | |

**3b** Compare your answers with a partner. What aspect of the speaker's intonation helped you to decide whether they were interested or not?

If you sound uninterested, you will find it difficult to maintain the interest of your audience. It will also be very difficult for the audience to follow your main arguments. Imagine a website without any bullet points, boxes, headings or different colours. It would be very difficult to find key words and information easily. Intonation does the job of those written features when we speak.

**3c** Work in groups of three. Take it in turns to read the sentences in 3a aloud, trying to use intonation to sound interested.

**3d** Work in pairs. Read aloud this extract from a question-and-answer session at the end of a presentation on the differences between laptops and desktop computers.

**A:** Does anyone have any questions?

**B:** Yes. You said that laptops occupied less space than a traditional computer, but modern desktop computers have become so much slimmer in recent years.

**A:** Well, yes, that's true. But you still have a lot of different parts, the keyboard, the main tower and the monitor, and they all take up space in a small home.

**B:** You didn't mention anything about security. If you put important, confidential information on a laptop, who knows what will happen if you lose it?

**A:** That's absolutely true. But did you know that laptop thefts reached an all-time low last year, and those that do disappear are usually password protected?

3.14

**3e** Listen to the dialogue and compare your intonation with the speakers', then read the dialogue aloud again.

## 4 Referring to visual materials

### Graphs, charts and diagrams

**3.15**

**4a** Listen to two descriptions of this chart showing the growth of wind power around the world. Which description (A or B) is easier to follow? Why?

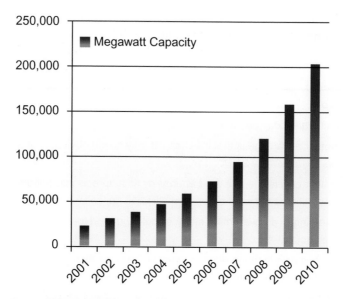

**Figure 1: Total world wind energy production (megawatts) (World Wind Energy Report, 2010)**

> When describing visual data, it is helpful to introduce the chart, give an overview, and remind people why you included the chart in your presentation. It isn't a good idea to read all the numbers on the chart. Choose key points to focus on and talk in detail about them.

**4b** Match the signpost phrases (1–5) in the table with their functions (a–e).

**a** Draw attention to the visual

**b** Give an overview of the information

**c** Highlight some interesting points

**d** Introduce what the visual shows

**e** Summarize the main point

| Function | Signpost phrases to refer to visual information |
| --- | --- |
| 1 ___[a]___ | *OK, could you all turn to page 2 on your handout and look at Figure 2?* |
| 2 _____ | *Well, you can see that, overall, the numbers have increased/decreased over the period.*<br>*There is a large difference in ...*<br>*As you can see, there are three main ...* |
| 3 _____ | *So what this means is that ...*<br>*This is significant because ...*<br>*So, you can see that ...* |

| 4 _____ | *The chart here gives an overview of the number of ...* |
| | *This diagram shows ...* |
| 5 _____ | *I think it's interesting to look at the figures for ...* |
| | *As you can see, there is a large gap between ...* |

**4c** Work in pairs. Look at these diagrams about the best location for a wind turbine and describe them to your partner. Use the signpost phrases in 4b.

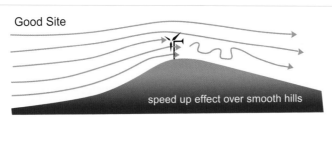

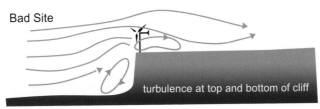

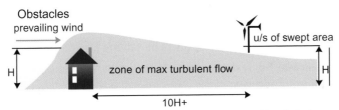

locate the turbine away from the turbulence caused by obstacles

Source of graphic: http://www.greenspec.co.uk/html/energy/windturbines.html

When presenting visual materials, speakers often follow these stages. Speakers may repeat one or more stages.

1  Draw attention to the visual.
2  Introduce what the visual shows in general, usually referring to the title.
3  Summarize the main message of the visual.
4  Highlight/Describe a trend or key point.
5  Support the key point using example data from the visual.
6  Give an overview of what the information means.

**4d** A student is presenting this chart to a group of students. Put the extracts from the presentation in the correct order, using the stages on p.141 to help you.

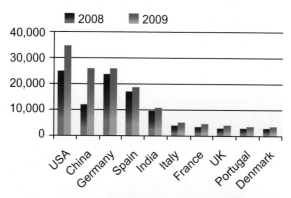

**Figure 2: Top ten countries total wind power production (megawatts)**

**a** As you can see, it gives an overview of the top-ten producers in terms of wind-generated power in both 2008 and 2009. _____

**b** OK, let's have a look at this graph which shows which countries produce the most wind power. ___1___

**c** At 35,000 megawatts per year in 2009, this is over 10,000 higher than their nearest rivals, China and Germany, who both produced around 25,000 megawatts. _____

**d** So what this suggests is that only five countries – the USA, China, Germany, Spain and India – were responsible for a huge proportion of the world's wind power. _____

**e** Interestingly, although both these countries had more or less the same production, this wasn't the case a year earlier. _____

**f** This clearly shows that the USA is by far the largest producer. _____

**g** China showed the fastest growth in this year, almost doubling its wind-generation production in one year. _____

**4e** Listen and check your answers.

3.16

**4f** Present the information in this chart to a partner. Use the language from 4d.

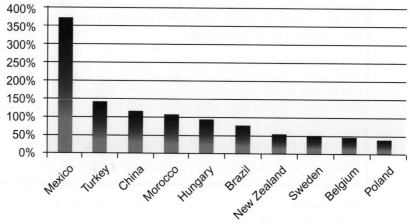

**Figure 3: Percentage increase in wind power generation, 2009**

**PowerPoint and overhead slides**

> If you choose to use PowerPoint slides, it is important to use them as a starting point for your presentation. They should be a summary of what you want to say, or present key supporting information. Never just read your slides aloud.

3.17

**4g** Listen to two students giving a presentation. Both are using the PowerPoint slide below. Which presentation is more interesting? Why?

## Advantages

✓ **Relatively cheap to run (Johnson, 2008)**
✓ **Very clean and environmentally friendly**
✓ **No risk of contamination (Department of Trade and Industry, 2009)**
✓ **Sustainable**

**4h** Look at this PowerPoint slide. Complete the presentation below with the introduction phrases from the list.

## Disadvantages

✗ **Unpopular with the general public – unattractive and noisy**
✗ **Intermittent supply (Department of Trade and Industry, 2009)**
✗ **Insufficient to power industry**

| | | |
|---|---|---|
| And finally, | Another major challenge is | ~~OK, let's turn now to~~ |
| So as you can see, | Well, the first challenge | |

_OK, let's turn now to_ the disadvantages of wind power. _____[1] is persuading the general public to accept the wind turbines in locations near their homes. _____[2] the problem of supply …

_____[3] there is the problem of industrial use. _____[4] there are still some valid concerns about the use of wind power.

**4i** Work in pairs. Read the statements (1–3) and decide where each statement could be added to the presentation.

1 You might think that the biggest issue here was a lack of wind, but actually, at the moment, many wind farms are being paid to switch their turbines off during very high winds, as the power generated is too high, and this has caused millions of pounds' worth of damage to electrical equipment.

**2** Although wind turbines can supply enough energy to heat our homes and light the streets, they can't generate the levels required to meet the energy requirements of a large factory.

**3** Many people feel that the wind turbines are an unattractive addition to the countryside. Those who live near wind turbine plants also complain that the noise levels are unacceptable.

3.18

**4j** Listen and check your answers.

> When you present PowerPoint slides, make sure you use suitable language to introduce the main points and make conclusions. Expand on the notes on the PowerPoint slide with supporting information and refer back to previous slides where appropriate.

> ▶ **LESSON TASK**   **5 Giving a presentation with visuals**

**5a** You are going to prepare and deliver a presentation with a partner using visual materials. Work in pairs. Read the project assignment about greenhouse gas emissions. Evaluate how well the UK has performed compared to its emissions targets.

> **Project assignment**
> In December 1997, the UK signed an agreement known as the Kyoto Protocol. This agreement set the UK the target of reducing greenhouse gas emissions by 12.5% from the 1990 figures by the year 2012. Consider whether the UK has done enough to improve its environmental record, and present this evidence with a partner to the group.

**5b** Study the two graphs below and answer these questions.

**1** Has the UK done enough to meet the targets set at Kyoto?

**2** Is there more the UK could do to improve its environmental record?

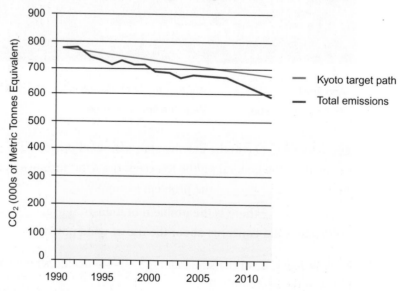

**Figure A: UK greenhouse gas emissions, 1990–2008 projected to 2012**

*Data source: United Nations Statistics Division (2011). Greenhouse Gas (GHGs) Emissions without Land Use, Land-Use Change and Forestry (LULUCF), in Gigagrams (Gg) $CO_2$ equivalent. Retrieved from: http://data.un.org/Data.aspx?q = + greenhouse + gas&d = GHG&f = seriesID%3aGHG*

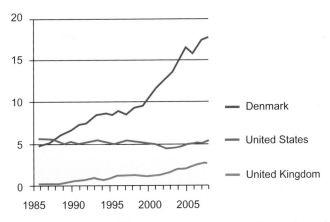

**Figure B: Renewable energy as a percentage of total energy supply**

*Data source: OECD (2010). OECD Factbook 2010: Economic, Environmental and Social Statistics. Paris: OECD. Retrieved from: http://www.oecd-ilibrary.org/economics/oecd-factbook-2010/contribution-of-renewables-to-energy-supply-table_factbook-2010-table124-en*

**5c** Work in pairs. Decide:

- how you are going to introduce the topic
- how you will organize the talk
- who will cover each different aspect of the topic.

**5d** Use these PowerPoint slides to prepare the first part of your presentation.

Slide 1

## Kyoto Protocol – 1997

- **targets global warming**
- **sets greenhouse gas emission reductions relative to 1990 levels**
- **UK goal – reduce emissions by 12.5% by 2012**

Slide 2

## UK performance in $CO_2$ reductions

- **reached Kyoto targets in late 1990s**
- **should achieve approx 13% reduction by 2012 – double original target**

## UK performance – renewable energy

- **slow to adopt this technology**
- **less than 5% of total energy generated by renewable sources**
- **Denmark – more than 6 times higher**

**5e** In your presentation you want to talk about the carbon dioxide produced when products are manufactured abroad but imported and used in the UK. Look at this information from an environmental report and create a draft slide on a spare piece of paper.

### The UK's carbon dioxide consumption rise

According to a new study produced by the Stockholm Environment Institute, the UK's carbon dioxide consumption actually rose between 1992 and 2004 if a different and more realistic system of measuring $CO_2$ consumption was used.

Under the terms of the Kyoto Protocol, the amount of $CO_2$ produced through manufacturing, domestic and transport use is measured only within the borders of individual countries. This means that many European countries, such as the UK, appear to have consequently seen a reduction in their $CO_2$ production, because of the trend towards relocating heavy industry abroad in recent years. This also means that countries such as China and Vietnam often have a poor $CO_2$ record, even though the goods they produce are not used to benefit the population in these nations.

However, if the Kyoto Protocol took into account the amount of carbon dioxide produced to create goods consumed by a nation, then the UK's $CO_2$ consumption increased overall by 18% between 1992 and 2004. This is equivalent to 115 million tonnes of $CO_2$.

Source: Sleat, P. & Wilson, M. (2010). Making Waves – Kyoto and the UK. Reading: Green Press Ltd.

**5f** Work in groups of four. Take turns to give your presentation. As one pair speaks, the other pair writes notes in this table.

|  | ☺ | ☹ | Comments |
|---|---|---|---|
| Was it clear when the talk moved from one stage to another? |  |  |  |
| Was the intonation lively and interesting? |  |  |  |
| Was the content clear enough? |  |  |  |
| Did the speakers expand on their visuals? |  |  |  |

## 6 Review and extension

### Using PowerPoint slides in a presentation

3.19

**6a** Listen to four extracts from a presentation on the relationship between universities and business and industry. Number the PowerPoint slides in the order you hear them used in the presentation.

A

> ## Overestimates the role of universities as sources of innovation
>
> - customers
> - suppliers
> - competitors
> - internal knowledge

B

> ## Business identifies less contractual relationship
>
> - provision of skilled staff
> - free access to conferences and publications
> - links to other agencies

C

> ## UK record
>
> - high performance – university science programmes
> - low performance – commercialization

## Knowledge economies based on STEM disciplines

- Science
- Technology
- Engineering
- Maths

### Using signposting expressions

**6b** Complete the presentation below by putting these phrases in the correct place.

> Hi, thanks for coming here today.
>
> I've divided my topic into three sections.
>
> Let me start by telling you what first interested me in this project.
>
> The main reason I'm here today is to talk about …
>
> This should only last ten minutes.

> *Hi, thanks for coming here today*. It's good to see so many familiar faces._____[1] a community energy project in the East District. It was a new scheme to get people to use a shared generator to power their homes. _____[2] There have been many schemes now in rural areas, where villagers have found it easier to set up their own mini-generators, using renewable energy sources, but this is the first one which uses the same principle in an urban environment. As so many people live in cities these days, this scheme offers very real possibilities to transform the way we create energy. _____[3] Firstly, I'm going to look at the barriers to setting up such a scheme in a town or city. Then we'll move on to some of the government support available. Finally, we'll look at the possibilities of copying this scheme in other places. _____[4], and then after that I hope to have time to answer any questions you have.

**6c** Complete the conclusion to the presentation in 6b using suitable phrases from the table on p.137.

> _____[1] there have been many benefits to this project. Although there were initial problems, the benefits once the scheme was set up outweigh these problems.
>
> _____[2] that local governments take the initiative and promote such schemes, with the provision of additional support in the earliest stages. _____[3] I would like to thank the people of the East District for their help in compiling this report, and thank you for your attention. _____[4]

# Reporting in writing

**By the end of Part E you will be able to:**

- report ideas from sources
- summarize information from other sources
- integrate information from sources into writing.

## 1 Reporting ideas from sources

**1a** Work in pairs. Match the quotations (1–3) with the people (a–c) who said them.

**a** Sarah Schmidt, a biologist writing in 2007

**b** Henry Dreyfus, an education specialist writing in 1900

**c** Roberto Albetti, a physicist writing in 2000

---

**1**

The discovery that electrons can exist in two different places at the same time suggests that things made of electrons can have two existences. All the more surprising when you consider that humans and the universe we live in are nothing but electrons.

---

**2**

The next century is going to see huge transformations in the field of bio-technology, changes in human engineering on a scale previously only possible in science fiction.

---

**3**

It is a mistake of modern society to treat science as separate subjects. What we know today is that biology is governed by the principles of chemistry, which in turn is subject to the rules of physics. We need to promote co-operation between the sciences, not discourage it.

---

**1b** Decide which quotation is:

**a** making a prediction     **b** offering an argument     **c** stating a fact.

### Reporting verbs

> Reporting verbs are used to tell the reader about what other sources have said on a topic. The type of reporting verb that you chose can indicate the function of the comment by the original source (for example, to make a prediction or claim, or to state a fact, etc.). The reporting verb that you chose can also show the reader whether you tend to agree with the source or not.

**1c** Match the words which have a similar meaning to *say* with the definitions (1–8).

| argue | claim | observe | point out | predict | ~~state~~ | suggest | warn |
|-------|-------|---------|-----------|---------|-----------|---------|------|

**1** say something factually true *state*

**2** say that something is true even though there may be no evidence _____

**3** say that something bad may happen _____

**4** mention something in order to give information or make the audience notice it _____

**5** give reasons why you think something is right/wrong or true/false _____

**6** put forward an idea or a plan for consideration _____

**7** say something you have seen or noticed during the course of research _____

**8** mention something that you think will happen in the future _____

**1d** Complete this paragraph by underlining the best verbs in bold.

> Animal rights activists have **argued** / **stated** that computer modelling makes the testing of drugs on animals unnecessary, and that tests cause suffering to animals, which is in fact illegal. However, the law **states** / **claims**[1] that it is illegal to cause unnecessary suffering to animals. An important question, therefore, is whether the suffering involved in testing drugs on animals is necessary. Some scientists **observe** / **warn**[2] that without being able to use animals in tests, it will be impossible to test new drugs safely. For instance, Smith (2007) **suggests** / **warns**[3] that animal rights activists' arguments against testing on live animals are based on a misunderstanding about the importance of safe medical research. Smith also **points out** / **warns**[4] that even though animals are used in trials, they are treated with the highest standards of care under the law and do not suffer unnecessarily. Such reassurance, however, is rarely accepted by campaigners for animal rights. A recent study by Marsh and Snyder (2010) attempted to analyze animal testing data over the last 30 years but found little clear evidence of its benefits. Furthermore, the authors **observed** / **warned**[5] that it is difficult to get accurate information about just how necessary animal testing actually is: 'Large drug companies **claim** / **observe**[6] that computer modelling isn't as effective as testing on live animals, but they present absolutely no evidence to support this.' (Marsh & Snyder, 2010, p.26).

### Tenses for reporting words

**1e** Look at the reported ideas in extracts a and b and then answer these questions for each extract.

**1** Which tense is used for the reporting words in bold?

**2** How long ago was the source author writing?

**3** Is the source author likely to still be writing today?

> **a** Einstein (1911) **predicted** that the light from a star would be bent by the sun's gravity. However, this phenomenon was only **reported** from observations following a solar eclipse many years later (Eddington, 1923).
>
> **b** Hawking (2008) **argues** that the existence of extra-terrestrial life is highly likely. However, he **points out** that primitive life is far more common than intelligent life, and the likelihood of finding intelligent life is still rare.

The tense used for reporting verbs can depend on a number of different factors. In general, reporting verbs are only used in the past if:

- the writer was writing a significantly long time ago (e.g. more than 40 years) and/or …
- their argument or viewpoint is generally accepted to have been replaced and/or …
- the writer using the source wants to report on a specific research study which took place in the past.

In almost all other cases, reporting verbs are used in the present.

## 2  Summarizing information from other sources

**2a**  Work in pairs. Try to think of advantages and disadvantages of using social networking sites.

**2b**  Read this text about social networking sites. Check whether any of your ideas in 2a are mentioned.

> I would argue that the use of social networking sites can lead to a number of related health problems, and there are several reasons for this. Firstly, the rise in the amount of time people are spending online, particularly young people, may be time they would otherwise be doing something active. It is well known that lack of exercise can contribute to a range of physical health problems. Secondly, spending so much time online may contribute to changes in the brains of young users. These changes have been linked to short attention spans and even increased incidences of autism (Barlow, 2008). I would also argue that spending large amounts of time on online social networking sites may encourage instant gratification and make young people more self-centred.
>
> Greenfield, S. (2009). *The New Society.* San Francisco: Mirage Publications

**2c**  Three different students have included this information in their essays in different ways. Match the ways of reporting information (1–3) with the students' work (A–C).

1 paraphrasing – using the same idea as the original author, but expressing it in different words; this is usually done for short pieces of text, for instance a phrase or a sentence

2 quoting – using the exact same words as the author

3 summarizing – explaining a writer's main idea briefly, in your own words; summaries usually condense the main idea from a larger amount of text into a few sentences

**A**

> Greenfield (2009) goes as far as to claim that 'spending large amounts of time on online social networking sites may encourage instant gratification and make young people more self-centred'. However, this is a difficult point to prove.

**B**

> Greenfield (2009) argues that there may be a connection between the frequent use of social networking sites for long periods of time and the levels of selfish behaviour shown among users. He also argues that these young people are more likely to desire results immediately.

**c**

> Greenfield (2009) claims that social networking sites may have a negative effect on emotional, physical and psychological development.

When you summarize an idea, you need to:

**1** represent the author's ideas accurately

**2** state the source of the idea clearly

**3** write in your own words.

It is not acceptable to select a few phrases from the original and copy them into a shortened sentence or paragraph.

**2d** Which of these sentences are <u>not</u> acceptable summaries of the ideas in the text in 2b? Why not?

**a** Greenfield (2009) has suggested spending long hours on social network sites can cause brain damage.

**c** Greenfield (2009) claims that overuse of the Internet may lead to physical changes in people's brains.

**b** Changes in young people's brains may occur if they spend a large amount of time on the Internet.

**d** According to Greenfield, spending increased amounts of time online contributes to changes in the brain (2009).

**2e** You are writing an essay on the applications of technology and have found this source. Read the text and underline the key information.

## How children socialize

The Teaching and Learning Research Programme launched their Technology Enhanced Learning Initiative this year. The aim of the project is to use interactive computer programs and equipment to learn more about how young children socialize. Children in the programme will be aged between five and seven. These are the ages when children first start to attend school and are faced with their first challenges socially. Computer equipment located in schools, after-school clubs and holiday workshops will be able to record the child's gaze, facial expression and gestures, using cameras and microphones. It is hoped that the findings will provide vital information on socialization, which might help to better understand autism and promote better learning environments. (Teaching and Learning Research Programme, 2010)

**2f** Work in pairs. Tell your partner what the main points were without looking at the extract.

**2g** Summarize the information in the text to support this point in your essay. **Use only one sentence**. Make sure you give the correct referencing information.

At present it is difficult to assess how far the use of computer technology affects children, although there are a number of ongoing research projects in this area. For example, _____

_____

_____

_____.

**2h** Work in pairs. Exchange summaries and make comments on the content and the language.

## 3 Integrating information from sources into writing

**3a** Work in small groups. Discuss these questions.

1 Do you shop online? Why / why not?

2 Which is safer – shopping online or shopping in a city centre? How?

3 Do you think emails are a secure form of communication? Why / why not?

4 Which is more secure – communicating by email or by post?

**3b** Read the extract below from a student's essay which includes a reference to another source. Are these sentences true (T), false (F) or not stated (NS)?

1 Evans argues that emails are normally a safe method of sending private information.

2 Evans suggests that emails can be accessed while you are writing them.

3 Evans believes that there are times when your emails can be accessed by others.

4 Evans states that information about your email account becomes available when you visit a website.

5 Evans claims that people who access emails in this way may have bad intentions.

> There are several risks associated with privacy when sending and receiving emails. Some of these are associated with the way the Internet is structured through a system of communication nodes using different servers. According to Evans (2001), when an email is sent or a browser is used to get access to a website, the chances of communication being intercepted among the millions of other similar communications travelling in cyberspace are infinitesimal. She suggests that the privacy risks actually begin when an email passes through a node on its way to its destination or is sitting on a server, because both can be hacked into by malicious people or criminals. Then, when you access a website, the server which carries your request will be logged and identified (Evans, 2001). In other words, your personal information is not well protected and can be stolen easily and may then be used for illegal purposes.

**3c** Underline the sentences of the paragraph in 3b which are the student's own work, i.e. **not** ideas paraphrased from the source.

> In your academic writing, it is important to make sure that ideas from sources do not look like isolated, disconnected phrases. When you use a source, it is a good idea to introduce it with a sentence written in your own words. You should also make a concluding remark when you have finished referring to the source.

**3d** Look at the **second** sentence of the paragraph in 3b. Why do you think the student decided to write this sentence? Discuss which of the following function(s) it has:

1 To give the main idea of the paragraph.

2 To give some background for the following paraphrasing from the source.

3 To help prepare the reader for the ideas the student uses in the source.

4 To give another point in the student's argument.

5 To link information to a previous paragraph.

**3e** Read this paragraph from another student essay on the same topic as that in 3b. Decide which of the sentences (1–3) would best fit the gap in the paragraph.

> *The threat to an individual's private information is very real, and it is therefore important to take steps to keep it safe. _____. As pointed out by Ryrie (2002), access to an email can be achieved by anyone with the right level of access to the server it is stored on, and he therefore suggests that perhaps the best way to reduce security risks is to encrypt the actual email. In other words, adding individual electronic passwords to an email before it goes out and before it reaches a server will probably be much more effective than server-based security measures.*

1 There are a number of ways of doing this, but the most effective way is one which matches the nature of the problem.

2 There are a number of different computer security products available, although many of these are quite expensive.

3 Governments around the world are becoming increasingly concerned by security threats.

**3f** Match these concluding remarks for the essay in 3e (1–5) with a function (a–f) in the table on p.155. Some of these remarks fulfil more than one function.

1 Perhaps the only way to reduce security risks is to encrypt the email; in other words, add passwords to the computer system. ___*b*___

2 So, as the evidence suggests, encryption is not a totally effective method. _____

3 In other words, if encryption systems are not used, large financial losses may result, which would be a disaster for many areas of computer-based business. _____

4 What is missing from this analysis of computer security is a consideration of the financial implications for small businesses. _____

5 If these problems are addressed, there is a possibility that computer hacking on a large scale can be avoided in future. _____

| Concluding remarks | |
|---|---|
| **Function** | **Example** |
| **a** summarize the ideas | *So as X argues, there may be little we can do without further investment from government or industry.* |
| **b** reach a conclusion | *This means that current data may not provide sufficient information.* |
| **c** assess the value of the source | *Y makes a valid point when s/he argues that ...* <br> *These results may not hold true if the experiment were repeated with a larger sample size.* |
| **d** offer a warning | *If what Z says is true, the consequences could be more serious than we thought.* |
| **e** make a prediction | *This suggests that there may be a solution emerging in the next few years.* |
| **f** refer to information in the following paragraph | *However, those who have argued in favour of solar power have not considered the environmental impact of manufacturing and disposing of the solar panels over their lifetime, which can outweigh any benefits during their use.* |

**3g** Write concluding remarks for the extracts from academic text books (A–C) below and on p.156 using the language in 3f.

*Example*

The speed of globalization and the growing links between countries have both increased at an ever faster pace in recent years. Beck (1999) coined the term 'Risk Societies' for the way we live in the modern world. The concept of risk societies was simple: in the past when heads of governments met, they were interested in negotiating 'good', things like access to education, income and medicine and trade rights. These days international negotiation has been characterized by 'bad', things such as responsibility for environmental damage, cross-border crime and global health risks.

*This suggests that there has been a fundamental change in the way we live, which looks likely to continue.*

**A**

The issue which has received the most attention is pollution and the dangers of global warming. The international nature of modern-day pollution was first observed in Sweden in the 1970s. Mallinson (1985) reports that in the 1970s, many square kilometres of forests in Sweden and other parts of Scandinavia were dying for inexplicable reasons. Gradually, studies of wind patterns across Northern Europe revealed that it was pollution from the heavily industrialized north of England blowing straight to the forests of Scandinavia, where it was killing the trees.

_____

_____

_____

**B**

If there was any need for further proof that we were now living in a global world, it came in the 1980s. In April 1986, an explosion at the Chernobyl Nuclear Power Station sent radioactive contamination around the planet. Unlike naturally occurring disasters, such as an earthquake or volcanic eruption, this explosion was not limited in either distance or time. According to the European Commission (2009), the effects of the Chernobyl nuclear disaster can still be measured in sheep farms in Wales over twenty years later and several thousand miles away. The World Health Organization (2005) estimated that fewer than fifty people died in the immediate explosion. However, it is more likely that in the following years and decades, many thousands more deaths occurred.

_____

_____

_____

**C**

Increased interdependency may also provide the solutions to, as well as the causes of, these problems. Thanks to the Internet, more research than ever is published and freely accessible to researchers working in related fields. Davies (2008) argued that this had undoubtedly been a key driving force behind the speed of change in modern societies. Although plans for international co-operation and a united effort to tackle cross-national problems such as pollution, disease and international crime are in their infancy, plans are underway and are beginning to have some impact.

_____

_____

_____

**3h** Compare your answers with a partner. Discuss the function of your concluding remarks.

> **LESSON TASK**   **4 Summarizing and reporting information**

**4a** You have been asked to write an academic essay discussing the possibility of using more nuclear power for the production of electricity. Work as a small group. Brainstorm some ideas and make notes in this table of some possible benefits and problems of using more nuclear power.

| Possible benefits of using nuclear power | Possible problems of using nuclear power |
| --- | --- |
|  |  |

**4b**  Your tutor will give you a source relating to the essay title. You will need to read this source and summarize it orally for the other students in your group using your own words. You will also need to decide on a suitable reporting verb to use.

**4c**  Share your ideas about the different sources and keep a record of the summaries of all the sources available by making notes of what other students tell you, using this sheet.

---

*Suggested reporting verbs:* question / demonstrate / suggest / claim / agree with / observe

*Summaries of source ideas/information:*

**Source A**



**Source B**



**Source C**



**Source D**


---

**4d**  Read these introductory sentences from two different paragraphs (A and B) from an essay about nuclear power. Decide which source(s) from 4c would be the most appropriate to support the point made in each sentence. Use the summary of the source(s) you have chosen to complete the paragraph.

**A**

There are persuasive arguments for using nuclear technology in energy production.

**B**

However, the use of nuclear technology remains highly controversial.

**4e** Work in groups. Read the paragraphs completed by the other students and use the evaluation questions below to help give the writers some feedback (**5** = excellent, **1** = much more work needed).

| Evaluation point | Rating | Comments |
|---|---|---|
| Suitable reporting verb used | 5  4  3  2  1 | |
| Accuracy of summarizing ideas from source | 5  4  3  2  1 | |
| Use of own words in summarizing | 5  4  3  2  1 | |
| Integration of summarizing | 5  4  3  2  1 | |
| Accuracy of referencing | 5  4  3  2  1 | |
| Accuracy of grammar/ vocabulary | 5  4  3  2  1 | |

## 5  Review and extension

### The language of research

**5a** Look at these sentences. Choose the best word to complete the sentences.

*Example*
*Scientists have looked for ice on the planet Mars as this would* <u>suggest</u> / **refute** *that the two chemicals necessary for life, hydrogen and oxygen, are present there.*

1 Newton created his theory of gravity by **warning** / **observing** that the planets did not fall out of the sky.

2 Einstein's rule of relativity *gives the* **impression** / **states** that $E = mc^2$.

3 Before the days of global travel, many 'scientists' **claimed** / **pointed out** that the Earth was flat.

4 A lot of modern-day evolutionists are discovering evidence which **disproves** / **observes** parts of Darwin's Theory of Evolution.

5 This research needs to be **refuted** / **validated** by an expert in the field.

6 The figures **indicate** / **state** that the ban on smoking in public places has had an effect on older smokers.

**5b** Match these words with their synonyms in the table.

agree with          question          show          suggest

| 1 _____ | 3 _____ |
|---|---|
| *contradict* | *illustrate* |
| *disprove* | *prove* |
| *refute* | *demonstrate* |

| 2 _____ | 4 _____ |
|---|---|
| *indicate* | *support* |
| *imply* | *back up* |
| *give the impression* | *validate* |

**5c** Complete these sentences with the correct form of the verbs from 5b. Not every synonym will necessarily work.

1 In his paper, Dr Pathetis _____ the traditional argument that calorie intake is the main cause of weight problems. He argues that changes in exercise are the cause.

2 It was _____ that the results of this case study were likely to be repeated in other schools around the country.

3 There is very little evidence in the report _____ their conclusion.

4 What this experiment _____ is that there is little relation between the two.

> Try to use the correct terminology and suitable academic reporting verbs when you mention original sources in your own essays or presentations.

**5d** Match the words or phrases in bold on the left (1–8) with their collocations on the right (a–h).

| | |
|---|---|
| 1 There is **growing** | a **inaccurate assumptions** about ... |
| 2 A **research project** which was | b **from the research** in the field ... |
| 3 They **make** | c **the reasons for** this. |
| 4 Professor Brown **makes a** | d **concern among** academics ... |
| 5 This is **evident** | e **on** the effects of ... |
| 6 Scientists have not yet **identified** | f **valid point**. |
| 7 The study **focuses** | g **among researchers** in the field ... |
| 8 There appears to be **a consensus** | h **carried out** in the United States ... |

## Unit overview

| Part | This part will help you to … | By improving your ability to … |
|------|------------------------------|--------------------------------|
| **A** | **Understand lectures** | • understand how linking words signpost an argument<br>• understand how discourse markers signpost an argument. |
| **B** | **Compare and paraphrase texts** | • use modifiers with comparatives and superlatives<br>• paraphrase using words with an opposite meaning<br>• understand how commas improve clarity. |
| **C** | **Identify text structure** | • make efficient notes<br>• use discourse markers to understand abstracts<br>• understand written discourse markers. |
| **D** | **Give a pair presentation** | • express the aims of a presentation using clauses of purpose<br>• understand differences between spoken and written academic English<br>• understand and use connected speech. |
| **E** | **Get your point across in writing** | • show your position using adverbs and adjectives<br>• make recommendations and give warnings in conclusions<br>• develop your writing style by varying the length of sentences. |

# Understanding spoken information

**By the end of Part A you will be able to:**

- understand how linking words signpost an argument
- understand how discourse markers signpost an argument.

## 1 Understanding how linking words signpost an argument

> A good lecturer will use language signposts to help you to follow their overall argument and pick out individual points better. The lecturer's choice of linking words, for example, can show the relationship between different ideas, perhaps indicating whether the lecturer is going to add a new idea or show contrast.

**1a** You are going to listen to an extract from a lecture about health expectancy. The lecturer asks the question *What's the difference between life expectancy and health expectancy?* Work in pairs. Discuss the question and write your answers below.

| Life expectancy | Health expectancy |
|---|---|
|  |  |

**1b** Listen to the extract and check your ideas.

4.1

**1c** Listen again. Complete the transcript using *or*, *and* and *but*.

OK, today we're going to look at the topic of health expectancy. Now, many of you have probably heard of life expectancy, which is a fairly common measure of how many years somebody is expected to live. So, at birth, you might have a life expectancy of 70 years, _____*or*_____ 59 years. It's how long, on average, people would live in your country _____[1] your community. OK, so what is the difference between life expectancy _____[2] health expectancy?

Well, in short, it's a difference between the quantity of your life _____[3] the quality of your life. Life expectancy tells you simply how many years you are likely to live, _____[4] it does not tell you how much health you will enjoy in that time. Now health expectancy, on the other hand, is a measure of the quality of your life. You may live to be, for example, 80 years old, _____[5] will you spend all of those 80 years being healthy, enjoying the same good health that you maybe had when you were a child _____[6] in your younger years?

> *Or, and* and *but* are examples of linking words. You can use *or* and *and* to link two nouns or two clauses within a sentence. You can use *but* to link two main clauses.
>
> ***Examples***
>
> *Health expectancy is different for <u>men</u> **and** <u>women</u>.*
>
> *Governments should take into account <u>quantity of life</u> **and** <u>quality of life</u>.*
>
> <u>*Medical advances have increased health expectancy in recent years*</u>, **but** <u>*the emergence of new diseases threatens to reverse this trend*</u>.

4.2

**1d** Listen to a conversation between two students about their grandparents' health. Did their grandparents enjoy good health throughout their lives?

**1e** Listen again and complete these extracts from the conversation using linking words.

*Example*

*My grandmother didn't live a very long life, <u>nor</u> did my grandfather.*

**1** I hardly knew them because I was only a child when they died, _____ I've spoken to my mother about their lives _____ it seems that their quality of life was excellent in many ways.

**2** They were healthy and independent, _____ I think they probably had a much better life than if they had lived longer and suffered ill health.

**3** They are quite young and fit, _____ my mother already worries about how we will take care of them if we need to.

**4** She will have to give up her job, _____ pay for some help …

**1f** Check your answers with a partner.

**1g** Complete this table using the linking words in 1e.

| Linking word | Used to: |
|---|---|
| 1 | link two contrasting words or phrases |
| 2 | introduce a result or consequence of the previous word or phrase |
| 3 | introduce an alternative word or phrase |
| 4 | introduce something that is true or exists despite the previous word or phrase |
| 5 | add a second negative word or phrase |
| 6 | add a second positive word or phrase |

> *Yet* can also be used to introduce contrasting information, although *yet* tends to be used with more surprising or contradictory information than *but*. Compare:
>
> *Some cancers are more prevalent in Western countries, **but** others are found with equal distribution worldwide.*
>
> *The French are thought to have very unhealthy diets, **yet** their health expectancy is amongst the best in Europe.*

**1h** Match the beginnings of these sentences (1–6) with the endings (a–f) and add an appropriate linking word from this list. There may be more than one possible answer.

| and | but | nor | or | so | yet |
|-----|-----|-----|-----|-----|-----|

**1** Women usually live longer than men,

**2** Better health expectancy may be due to a healthy lifestyle

**3** Health expectancy is different in every continent,

**4** Most people wouldn't want to live a long but unhealthy life,

**5** Scotland has a lower life expectancy than England

**6** Many people are aware of the concept of 'life expectancy',

**a** _____ because of genetic factors.

**b** _____ they are likely to spend more time suffering from ill health later in life.

**c** _____ a slightly lower health expectancy too.

**d** _____ it seems that culture and ethnicity may influence it.

**e** _____ it is health expectancy which actually indicates a better quality of life.

**f** _____ would they wish to live with a serious disability.

> Notice how *nor* is slightly different from the other linking words. In the phrase after *nor*, the order of the subject and auxiliary verb is reversed.
>
> Two separate sentences:
>
> 1 subject   2 verb                                        1 subject   2 verb
> *Most people wouldn't* want to live a long but unhealthy life. *They wouldn't* wish to live with a serious disability either.
>
> One phrase joined with *nor*:
>
> 1 subject   2 verb                                        1 verb   2 subject
> *Most people wouldn't* want to live a long but unhealthy life, nor *would they* wish to live with a serious disability.

**1i** Listen to the first half of six extracts (1–6) from a lecture on health and write the linking words you hear.

4.3

| First half of extracts | Ideas to complete the extract |
|---|---|
| 1 Many overweight people blame their condition on their genes, —————— … | |
| 2 Living a healthy lifestyle doesn't mean exercising for two hours every day, —————— … | |
| 3 You may find exercise more fun if you do something you enjoy, like dance, —————— … | |
| 4 To lose weight, most doctors agree that you need to exercise regularly —————— … | |
| 5 Studies suggest that you should exercise for at least 30 minutes to see positive effects, —————— … | |
| 6 It is widely known that smoking and drinking excessively are bad for our health, —————— … | |

**1j** Work in pairs. Predict what kind of information might follow on from each extract. Make notes in the table in 1i.

**1k** Listen to each complete extract and take notes. Then compare your predictions in 1j with what the lecturer actually says.

4.4

**1l** Work in pairs. Discuss the extent to which you agree with the lecturer's claims.

## 2 Understanding how discourse markers signpost an argument

As well as linking words, lecturers also use *discourse markers* as signposts for the listener. Discourse markers are the words or phrases that the speaker uses to sequence, focus and clarify their speech. Discourse markers are often unplanned, occurring when the speaker pauses to think, for example, or takes an unexpected direction.

*Examples*

*Some examples are, **well**, **let's see**, introducing healthier options for school dinners or in work canteens.* (the lecturer uses *well* and *let's see* to give herself time to think of an example)

*Studies have shown that children's concentration improves dramatically when they eat a more nutritionally balanced breakfast. **Besides**, healthy breakfast options are often cheaper than many sugary children's favourites.* (the lecturer uses *besides* to show that they are going to add another point supporting their argument – here the cost benefits as well as the health benefits)

Discourse markers can have a number of different functions depending on the context.

**2a** Work in pairs. Discuss why the discourse marker *OK* is used in these situations (1–3).

*Example*

*We need to move towards a more complex definition of health, OK?*

*OK* is used here to seek agreement.

1 OK, are you ready to get started?

2 Today we've discussed life expectancy and health expectancy: the differences between the two and their usefulness in determining government policy. OK, that's it – do you have any questions?

3 **Doctor:**  You should start exercising gradually.

  **Patient:**  OK.

  **Doctor:**  And work up to a programme where you're doing thirty minutes per day, three or four times per week.

### Signposts used to indicate the start of a new point

4.1

**2b** Listen to the extract from the lecture on health expectancy in 1b (p.161) again. Which of the words and phrases in bold is *not* used to indicate the start of a new point?

> **OK**, today we're going to look at the topic of health expectancy. **Now**, many of you have probably heard of life expectancy, which is a fairly common measure of how many years somebody is expected to live. So, at birth, you might have a life expectancy of 70 years, or 59 years. It's how long, on average, people would live in your country or your community. **OK, so** what is the difference between life expectancy, and health expectancy?
>
> **Well**, in short, it's a difference between the quantity of your life and the quality of your life. Life expectancy tells you simply how many years you are likely to live, but it does not tell you how much health you will enjoy in that time. **Now** health expectancy, on the other hand, is a measure of the quality of your life. You may live to be, for example, 80 years old, but will you spend all of those 80 years being healthy, enjoying the same good health that you maybe had when you were a child or in your younger years?

**2c** You are going to listen to an extract from another lecture advising students on living healthily. Work in pairs. Predict the advice you think the lecturer may give. Write notes below.

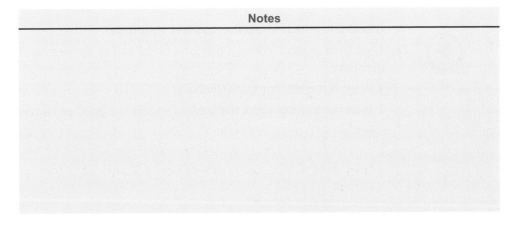

Notes

**2d** Listen and check your answers.

**2e** Listen again and read the transcript. Underline three expressions that the lecturer uses to start new points.

4.5

> All right, what about doing regular exercise on a budget? Well, keeping fit isn't only about joining expensive gyms or buying the latest fitness equipment. In fact, there are many ways of exercising without spending any money at all, like walking to college rather than taking the bus, or playing a team sport in the park with friends. Incidentally, university sports clubs, while they may ask you to pay a small fee, are often much cheaper than practising the same sport privately. Let's also remember that a lot of sporting gear can be bought second-hand, though this isn't a good idea if you're buying equipment where safety is premium.
>
> Right, we've talked about the importance of diet and physical well-being, but how many of you have thought about your mental health? Many students rely on stimulants such as caffeine and sugar to maintain their energy levels during the day but are unaware that after the initial energy boost, they experience a crash which often does enough harm to undo any positive effect. This crash may make studying very hard, in particular if a long period of concentration is required, for example in a lecture or an exam. And drinking too much caffeine and sugar, by the way, of course can lead to other physical problems and greater ill health in the long term.

**Signposts used before an unexpected change of topic**

> During a lecture the speaker may *digress*, or discuss topics which are slightly off the main point. These are usually still connected to the overall theme of the lecture and may still be worth writing down in your notes. However, some speakers may interrupt their lectures with stories or jokes. Recognizing these digressions will help you judge the relevance of points.

**2f** Look at the transcript in 2e again. Underline the discourse marker

1 in the first paragraph which indicates a change of topic from *exercise can be free* to *exercise can be made cheaper*

2 in the second paragraph which indicates a change in focus from study to health.

**Signposts which show the speaker's attitude**

**2g** Listen to a student asking a question at the end of the lecture and answer these questions.

4.6

1 What is the student worried about?

2 Does the lecturer think the student's habit is a good or bad one?

**2h** Listen again and underline discourse markers used by the speaker(s). These may be quite obvious expressions of opinion, or more subtle words which suggest the speaker's level of agreement/certainty, etc.

> **Student:** Can you repeat what you said about drinking coffee? I have four or five cups a day and I always thought it helped me study, so, to be honest, I'm quite worried!
>
> **Lecturer:** Drinking coffee – or consuming any other stimulant – does cause an increase in alertness for a short period of time. However, just as your body reacts to the drug as it kicks in, it reacts as it wears off, so you feel less alert than you would normally. This either means that you have to continue taking the stimulant, leading to addiction and in some cases overreaction – I mean, don't you ever feel strange after so much coffee? – or, more often, that your concentration simply suffers an hour or so later.
>
> **Student:** So really, if I have a cup of coffee in the morning before the exam, I'll actually perform worse during the exam because of it?
>
> **Lecturer:** Exactly. Frankly, I think that this is a much stronger argument for avoiding stimulants than any negative effect that they have on your physical health, at your age at least.

**2i** Complete this table using the discourse markers from this section.

| Function | Discourse markers |
|---|---|
| Starting a new point | Now, ... |
| Changing topic unexpectedly | |
| Showing the speaker's attitude | |

**2j** Compare your list with a partner.

**3 Using linking words and discourse markers**

**3a** Work in small groups. Write down six pieces of advice about diet and health. Keep the advice short and simple and do not use any linking words.

*Examples*
*Try to eat a variety of fruit.*
*Don't forget that vegetables are important as well.*

**3b** Work in small groups. Exchange your pieces of advice with another group. Combine two pieces of advice in a single sentence using an appropriate linking word from Section 1. Where this is not possible, add a linking word to the piece of advice and write a logical ending.

*Examples*

*Try to eat a variety of fruit **but** don't forget that vegetables are important as well.*

*Try to eat a variety of fruit. **However**, remember that fruit contains a lot of sugar, so you shouldn't eat too much.*

**3c** Share your advice with your classmates.

**3d** Plan a two-minute presentation, arguing your opinion on one of these questions:

  **1** What is the best diet for a new student living alone for the first time?

  **2** What combination of diet and lifestyle is the best way to avoid insomnia?

  **3** What lifestyle habits should students adopt in order to ensure that they are successful at university?

**3e** Work in groups. Deliver your presentation to your group. Use linking words and discourse markers to help structure your argument.

## 4 Review and extension

### Linking words

**4a** Match the sentence halves about school meals (1–7 and a–g) using an appropriate linking word. You will need to use some words more than once.

| and | nor | or | so |
|-----|-----|----|----|

| | |
|---|---|
| **1** Concentration can be affected by foods containing caffeine | **a** a free vegetable in school each day. |
| **2** New standards in school lunches mean that both the nutritional quality of the meals is controlled | **b** will they offer unhealthy snacks in the school shop at break times. |
| **3** Many parents prefer making their children packed lunches for school | **c** they know exactly what their child is eating. |
| **4** Some schools claim that they will no longer serve fast food, | **d** that quantities of fried foods are limited. |
| **5** Some primary schools take part in a scheme where pupils are offered either one piece of free fruit | **e** those with a high sugar content. |

| 6 | Parents usually have to decide between paying for their child to have school meals | f | do those whose annual income is lower than a certain level. |
| 7 | Parents who are not working do not have to pay for school meals, | g | preparing them a packed lunch at home. |

### Discourse markers (1): review

4.7

**4b** Listen to the first part of six extracts from another lecture about health. Write the discourse markers you hear in the second column of this table.

| Extract | Discourse marker | Following information |
|---|---|---|
| 1 Why, then, are school children's diets so important to health expectancy? | | a habits, likes and dislikes acquired during childhood will influence the rest of that child's life. <br> b moving on to my second point regarding the importance of proper exercise on a regular basis … |
| 2 What parents eat has a strong influence on what their children eat and enjoy eating. | | a in many cases these eating habits can cause a number of problems. <br> b but what about the other factor – exercise. How important is that? |
| 3 Cultural factors may also, then, be a factor where exercise is concerned. | | a I'll now move on to look at age … <br> b society needs to do more … |
| 4 The right kind of exercise is also important. | | a your heart rate needs to increase significantly during exercise. <br> b did you know that the local gym offers cheap rates for students? |
| 5 Of course, offering a variety of sports in schools requires equipment and training. | | a the government has introduced a new physical education programme. <br> b the way in which schools allocate their money to different things is complex. |
| 6 Regular physical exercise, not to mention working as a team, can therefore improve pupils' performance in the classroom. | | a teamwork skills in particular are much appreciated in the workplace as well … <br> b research suggests pupils' classroom performance improves by up to 25% in some cases … |

**4c** Work in pairs. Discuss which information (a or b) is more likely to follow the discourse markers you have written in the table.

**4d** Listen to the complete extracts and check your answers.

4.8

### Discourse markers (2): extension – returning to the main topic

When a speaker changes the topic unexpectedly, they will often use discourse markers to indicate that they are returning to the main topic.

4.9

**4e** Listen to another extract from the lecture on life and health expectancy.
Answer these questions.

    **1** What effect did disease have in the nineteenth century?

    **2** Which South American country does the lecturer mention?

    **3** Who was affected by the diseases the lecturer mentions?

**4f** Listen again. The discourse marker *incidentally* is used to change the subject.
Which discourse marker is used to return to the main subject? Check your answer
with the transcript (**Appendix 3**).

### Discourse markers (3): extension – clarifying a point

> Lecturers often restate or repeat ideas in order to clarify them.
>
> ***Example***
>
> *Medical advances are the main reason for improved life expectancy nowadays.*
> ***In other words**, two hundred years ago – or in fact much less – people often died
> from diseases which are now easily cured.*
>
> The discourse marker *in other words* shows that the lecturer is about to repeat
> their point. Being able to recognize these in a lecture will enable you to fully
> check that you understand the lecturer's point.

**4g** You are going to listen to another extract from the lecture on life and health
expectancy over time, in which the lecturer talks about the relationship between
access to food, and health, two hundred years ago. Work in pairs. Try to predict
what the speaker will say.

4.10

**4h** Listen and check your ideas.

**4i** Listen again. This time, focus on the language used to indicate that the lecturer is
about to restate a point. Write down any phrases you hear.

    **1** that _____

    **2** what _____

    **3** I _____

    **4** to _____

**4j** Check your answers with the transcript (**Appendix 4**).

### Discourse markers (4): record keeping

**4k** Make a section for recording discourse markers in your personal vocabulary
logbook, organized according to function. Include the functions you studied in this
unit and leave space for other functions.

**Unit 4**

**Part B**

# Understanding written information

**By the end of Part B you will be able to:**

- use modifiers with comparatives and superlatives
- paraphrase using words with an opposite meaning
- understand how commas improve clarity.

## 1 Using modifiers with comparatives and superlatives

**1a** You have been asked to write an academic report comparing the factors that contribute to health expectancies in two different countries. Work with other students and discuss the different health expectancies in your country compared to what you know about the UK.

**1b** One writer has decided to compare the health expectancies of the UK and New Zealand and has found these sources. Read the three extracts and answer the questions (1–3) below.

**A**

> Recent years have seen a fall in the New Zealand suicide rate overall, although it has a higher rate of suicide by young people than many other OECD countries.
>
> *Adapted from: Ministry of Social Development (2010). Social Report 2010. Wellington:*
> *New Zealand Ministry of Social Development.*

**B**

> In 2006, the estimated health expectancy – or independent life expectancy (ILE) – at birth stood at 67.4 years for New Zealand males and slightly higher, at 69.2 years, for females.
>
> *Adapted from: Ministry of Social Development (2010). Social Report 2010. Wellington:*
> *New Zealand Ministry of Social Development.*

**C**

> Residents in England enjoy much better health expectancies overall than in the other nations of the UK. (Smith et al., 2008, p.78)

**1** In extract A, how much higher is the rate of suicide among young people in New Zealand compared to other OECD countries?

   **a** a lot   **b** a little   **c** it isn't clear

**2** In extract B, how much higher is the health expectancy of women compared to men?

   **a** a lot   **b** a little   **c** it isn't clear

**3** In extract C, how much better is the health expectancy of English people compared to residents of the UK's other nations?

   **a** a lot   **b** a little   **c** it isn't clear

> You can use words and phrases called *modifiers* with comparatives to make them stronger or weaker.
>
> ***Examples***
>
> *Rates of heart disease are often <u>much</u> more prevalent in industrial societies.*
>
> *Health expectancy in Mediterranean countries is <u>slightly</u> higher than in the UK.*

**1c**  Underline the modifiers in the extracts which helped you answer the questions in 1b.

**1d**  You are going to read an extract from a student's essay on the effect of smoking on health expectancy. Work in small groups. Discuss what information you would expect to read about. Write notes of your ideas below.

| Notes |
| --- |
|  |

**1e**  Read the extract. Were your predictions correct?

Regular smoking is now widely known to have a far greater impact on health than early studies showed. The long-term effects are perhaps rather more worrying than the short-term for many. Those smoking more than twenty cigarettes a day are considerably more likely to suffer from heart and lung disease later in life, and most will die somewhat sooner than their non-smoking counterparts (Barrowby, 1998). However, the distant nature of these consequences may be one of the reasons many young smokers do not quit the habit. These young smokers should therefore bear in mind that already they are a lot more likely to have to visit a doctor than their non-smoking friends. Their lungs are quite a bit weaker, their heart rate is a little faster, and even their emotional well-being is thought to be a bit less stable (Grange & Spearman, 2005).

**1f**  Underline all the modifiers in the extract.

**1g**  Check your answers with a partner.

**1h**  The student in the essay in 1e has used some rather informal modifiers, which would not usually be found in academic writing. Find and replace these modifiers with their more formal equivalents.

## 2  Paraphrasing using words with an opposite meaning

> It can sometimes be effective to paraphrase by changing phrasing from positive to negative.
>
> ***Example***
> *It is **seldom easy** to collect reliable data.*
> *It is **often difficult** to collect reliable data.*

### Using antonyms (words with an opposite meaning)

**2a**  Work in pairs. Discuss how these factors negatively affect a person's health. Write notes below.

**1** lack of education

**2** low income

**3** poor accommodation

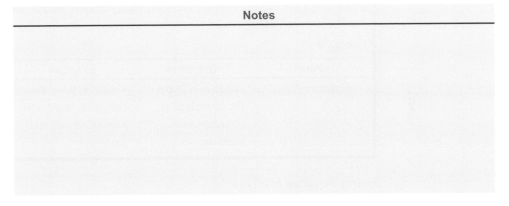

Notes

**2b**  Compare the extract below from a report on health expectancy in New Zealand with the notes a student made on it. Underline the words in the original text that the student has changed in her notes.

**Original text**

> Poor health is likely to emerge from lack of education, low income, and poor accommodation.
>
> *Adapted from: Ministry of Social Development (2010). Social Report 2010. Wellington: New Zealand Ministry of Social Development.*

**Student's notes**

> higher education, high income, good housing = good health

> The student has used *antonyms* to paraphrase the original text, words which have an opposite meaning to the original word.
>
> ***Examples***
> *low/high income*
> *poor accommodation/good housing*

**2c** Match the adjectives in bold (1–8) with their antonyms (a–h).

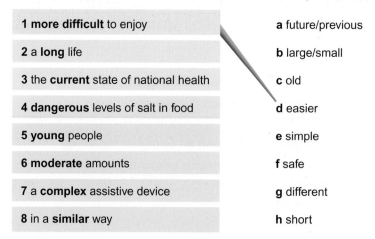

| | |
|---|---|
| **1 more difficult** to enjoy | **a** future/previous |
| **2** a **long** life | **b** large/small |
| **3** the **current** state of national health | **c** old |
| **4 dangerous** levels of salt in food | **d** easier |
| **5 young** people | **e** simple |
| **6 moderate** amounts | **f** safe |
| **7** a **complex** assistive device | **g** different |
| **8** in a **similar** way | **h** short |

> It is a good idea to note down any antonyms of new words you learn in your vocabulary logbook.
>
> *Example*
>
> | Word | Definition | Example | Antonym |
> |---|---|---|---|
> | appropriate (adj.) | suitable or right for a particular situation or occasion | I didn't think his comments were very appropriate at the time. | inappropriate (adj.) |

### Using negative prefixes

**2d** Work in pairs. Write a short definition of the term *successful ageing*.

**2e** Read this definition of successful ageing. To what extent does it match your own opinion?

> It is, perhaps, not surprising that the way an individual lives can affect their state of health in old age. *Successful ageing* can be defined as remaining healthy despite growing older, by adopting a lifestyle which promotes health well into old age. This includes such things as eating well, exercising, avoiding smoking and maintaining a positive attitude. It is not very likely that an individual who chooses to smoke, eat junk food and avoid exercise will be able to enjoy a healthy old age. (Hale, 2004, p.206)

**2f** Look at a student's notes on the text in 2e. Underline the words in the original text that the student has paraphrased.

> Hale (2004, p.206) claims = unsurprising that lifestyle affects health in old age.
> If unhealthy behaviour (smoking, no exercise, etc.) then healthy old age = unlikely.

> A prefix is a group of letters which can be added to the beginning of an existing word to change its meaning. A negative prefix changes the meaning to the opposite of the original word.
>
> **Example**
>
> un- + important = unimportant
>
> The two most common prefixes are *un-* and *in-*.
>
> Remember to make a note of any antonyms formed with negative prefixes when you record a new word in your personal vocabulary logbook.

**2g** Underline the places in the notes in 2f where the student has used a negative prefix as part of a paraphrase of Hale's ideas.

**2h** Complete this table with antonyms formed with *un-* or *in-*. Check your answers in a dictionary.

| Adjective/adverb without prefix | Antonym formed with negative prefix |
|---|---|
| **1** *surprising* (adj) | unsurprising |
| **2** *successfully* (adv) | |
| **3** *significant* (adj) | |
| **4** *active* (adj) | |
| **5** *correct* (adj) | |
| **6** *expected* (adj) | |
| **7** *common* (adj) | |
| **8** *sensitive* (adj) | |
| **9** *appropriate* (adj) | |
| **10** *popular* (adj) | |
| **11** *considerable* (adj) | |

**2i** Read an extract from a student's report on healthcare provision for the elderly. Underline the words with the negative prefixes *im-*, *il-* and *ir-*.

> In some regions programmes have been introduced to encourage the elderly to exercise regularly. Designing such programmes requires a high level of expertise. As the elderly are generally at greater risk from exercise, and can suffer from irregular health profiles, it would be irresponsible to allow participants to join a programme without consulting a medical professional. Even when a programme has been designed specifically for the elderly, potential participants are usually required to produce a medical certificate. It is, in fact, illegal for an exercise provider to allow participants to start exercising without being fully aware of any dangers.

Care must also be taken to ensure that the experience of exercise is a positive one. It is illogical to spend large amounts of money developing programmes if the programmes do not attract participants. Participants in some programmes complained that they found the level of medical questioning impolite, or that accessing facilities was impractical for those with limited mobility and finances.

**2j** Work in pairs. Discuss what the rules for using *im-*, *ir-* and *il-* might be.

> When you paraphrase, use antonyms and negative prefixes in conjunction with other techniques, such as using synonyms and changing from active to passive. Remember that not every word has an antonym, and that negative prefixes often cannot be added or removed. As you read and make notes on academic texts, notice adjectives and adverbs and think about their opposite meanings.

**2k** Underline words in this report which could be replaced with antonyms.

> In Europe today, six of the seven biggest risk factors for premature death relate to how we eat, drink and move. These include inadequate fruit and vegetable intake, physical inactivity and overuse of alcohol. Rising overweight and obesity across Europe is particularly worrying. (The European Commission, 2010)

**2l** Write a paraphrase of relevant parts of the text in 2k to support this point. Replace some of the words you have identified with antonyms.

*The increased levels of obesity in the developed world cannot be ascribed to a single cause.*

_____

_____

_____

## 3 Understanding how commas improve clarity

**3a** Read an extract from Weigand's article on successful ageing below. Say whether these statements are true (T) or false (F).

**1** The aim of ageing successfully is to live free from disability and disease for as long as possible.

**2** Recent studies suggest that fewer people are now freer from disability for longer.

> Perhaps **unsurprisingly**, there has been renewed interest in the idea of encouraging people to 'age successfully' – **that is**, to maintain healthy behaviours throughout life, **particularly in middle adulthood**, to experience as much of one's lifetime as possible free from serious disease or disability. There is some debate about whether increases in longevity mean an overall improvement of human life, or mean that **morbidity, disability, and serious illness** are merely 'put off' until later (Mor, 2005). **However**, several recent studies indicate that improvements in medical care and a shift in the types of illness which afflict the elderly mean that more people now enjoy a greater portion of their life free from serious disability.
>
> Source: Weigand, M. (2008). Towards a definition of 'successful ageing'. *Journal of Wellbeing*, 2, 238–239.

**3b** Look at the sections in bold in the extract in 3a. Identify which function(s) the commas serve, using this list.

| Possible functions of commas |
| --- |
| **A** To help highlight and clarify discourse markers. |
| **B** To separate additional (often less important) information from the main points. |
| **C** To separate items in lists. |

**3c** Now use what you have learnt to put commas in this academic text about future health trends in the UK.

In the current period the health status of the United Kingdom is comparable to that of other OECD nations and counterparts in the EU. However obesity levels which declined throughout the 1990s have been rising swiftly since the mid-1990s (NHSIC 2006 p.4). This does not equate to an immediate decline in healthy life expectancy as the negative physical and psychological impacts of morbid obesity take years to emerge across the population as a whole. It is to be expected that if current trends in obesity continue the gains made in other areas of health may be reduced within the next two decades. This prediction however does not account for the fact that medical advances in the coming years may push health expectancy up despite risk behaviours such as poor diet or overconsumption.

> **LESSON TASK**  **4 Improving the clarity of your writing**

**4a** As part of your university course, you have been asked to write a summary of a report comparing life expectancy in the UK now and thirty years ago. Work in small groups. Discuss and write notes on how you think life expectancy may have changed in the UK in that time.

| Notes |
| --- |
|  |

**4b** Compare your notes in 4a with this student's summary of the report.

> Life expectancy at birth which is the average number of years a newborn can expect to live is higher now than at any point in the UK's history. Unsurprisingly given historical trends, life expectancy for female newborns is higher than for male newborns but interestingly the difference between female and male life expectancy is getting smaller. One of the most positive developments in the last thirty years is that more people now live past the age of 65. Indeed where life expectancy is calculated from 65 rather than from birth, men and women will both live longer (by almost 20 years). Finally there are regional variations in UK life expectancy. The English can expect to live longer than the Welsh Northern Irish or Scottish, whether newborn life expectancy is used or life expectancy is calculated from 65.
>
> Source: National Statistics Online (2010). Life Expectancy [online]. Retrieved 22/06/2010 from http://www.statistics.gov.uk/cci/nugget.asp?id=168.

**4c** The tutor made comments on the student's report, highlighting any areas that needed to be changed.

Work in small groups. Correct and rewrite the underlined sections in the summary. The tutor's notes for the first six points are provided to help you. Think about the student's use of modifiers, antonyms and commas.

> Life expectancy at <u>birth which is the average number of years a newborn can expect to live</u>[1] is higher now than at any point in the UK's history. <u>Unsurprisingly</u>[2] given historical trends, life expectancy for female newborns <u>is higher</u>[3,4] than for male <u>newborns but interestingly</u>[5] the difference between female and male life expectancy is getting smaller. One of the most positive developments in the last thirty years is that <u>more people</u>[6] now live past the age of 65. <u>Indeed</u>[7] where life expectancy is calculated from 65 rather than from birth, men and women will both <u>live longer</u>[8] (by almost 20 years). <u>Finally</u>[9] there are regional variations in UK life expectancy. The English can expect <u>to live longer than</u>[10] the <u>Welsh Northern Irish or Scottish</u>[11], <u>whether newborn life expectancy is used or life expectancy is calculated from 65</u>[12].
>
> 1 Punctuation!
> 2 Comment adverb / discourse marker?
> 3 Can you use an antonym of 'higher' and rephrase this?
> 4 Can you express the degree of difference? Female life expectancy was 81.6 years and male 77.4 – large? small?
> 5 This long sentence needs at least one comma!
> 6 Degree of difference? Male mortality below 65 has dropped from 26% to 15% (this is quite considerable in 30 years, don't you think?) but female mortality from 16% to 10%.

**4d** Compare your rewritten text with another group. Did they make the same changes? Where they made different changes, do you think theirs were more or less successful than yours? Why? / why not?

## 5  Review and extension

### Using modifiers with comparative structures

**5a** Look at the notes on p.179, which a student took from a survey on sleep deprivation among students. Complete the sentences (1–4) using a modifier and the comparative form of the adjective in brackets.

| Sleep quality among male students | Sleep quality among female students |
| --- | --- |
| • Average sleep satisfaction rating (out of 10): first-year students 7, second-year 4, third-year 4 | • Average sleep satisfaction rating (out of 10): first-year students 3, second-year 4, third-year 5 |
| • Reporting serious sleep problems: first-year students 11%, second-year 15%, third-year 14% | • Reporting serious sleep problems: first-year students 25%, second-year 17%, third-year 14% |
| • Main cause of disturbed sleep: socializing 56%, worry about exams 16%, financial worries 6%, other 22% | • Main cause of disturbed sleep: socializing 49%, worry about exams 32%, financial worries 11%, other 8% |

### Example
*Male students' sleep satisfaction is <u>considerably</u> <u>higher</u> (high) than female students' in the first year.*

1 Socializing accounts for a _____ _____ (great) proportion of male students' sleep problems than any other cause.

2 Second-year female students' sleep satisfaction is _____ _____ (low) than in their third year.

3 A _____ _____ (large) proportion of female first-year students suffer sleep problems than males in the same year.

4 Sleeping well may be _____ _____ _____ (difficult) for female students overall.

### Using modifiers with *as ... as ...*

In Part B of Unit 1, you learnt how *as ... as ...* structures are used to show how two things are the same.

#### Example
*Third-year male students are as satisfied with their sleep quality as second-year male students.*

Modifiers can also be used with these structures.

**5b** Read this extract from a text discussing the health effects of lack of sleep. Does the fact that female students sleep less mean that their health suffers more? Why do you think this might be?

Female students also found their health was just as affected by sleep problems as male students: they were equally as likely to report difficulty concentrating after poor sleep in the short term, quite as likely to feel irritable after a poor night's sleep, and almost as likely to suffer headaches following a night of insomnia. The long-term risk of depression was also judged to be nearly as high as for male students if the students continued their current sleep habits.

**5c** Underline the modifiers used with *as ... as ...* in the extract in 5b. Write the modifiers in the correct column in this table.

| Modifiers showing that two things are exactly the same | Modifiers showing that two things are nearly the same |
| --- | --- |
| exactly as ... as ... | nearly as ... as ... |

**5d** Use the information in these notes from the same survey about student sleep patterns to complete the sentences (1–5) using a different modifier for each sentence.

| Sleep patterns among male students | Sleep patterns among female students |
| --- | --- |
| • 56% regularly experienced sleep problems on at least one day per week | • 62% regularly experienced sleep problems on at least one day per week |
| • 45% regularly experienced sleep problems on at least two days per week | • 45% regularly experienced sleep problems on at least two days per week |
| • 70% were unaware of advice about good sleeping habits | • 66% were unaware of advice about good sleeping habits |
| • 3% suffer chronic insomnia | • 3% suffer chronic insomnia |
| • 25% try to get extra sleep before exams | • 25% try to get extra sleep before exams |

1 Men were _____ as likely as women to regularly experience sleep problems on at least one day per week.

2 Women were _____ as likely as men to regularly experience sleep problems on at least two days per week.

3 Women were _____ as likely as men to be unaware of advice about good sleeping habits.

4 Men are _____ as likely as women to suffer chronic insomnia.

5 Women are _____ as likely as men to try to get extra sleep before exams.

**Using antonyms and negative prefixes**

**5e** Complete these sentences using an antonym of the word in brackets. Add or remove a negative prefix where possible.

1 Untroubled sleep is increasingly _____ (common) in the UK, prompting long-term health expectancy fears.

2 The phenomenon is widespread. It is slightly more common in _____ (rich) areas.

3 However, it is also a _____ (minor) problem in wealthier regions.

**4** The government has researched a number of _____ (impossible) solutions to the problem.

**5** Unfortunately, these solutions are by no means _____ (complex).

**5f** Paraphrase these sentences using antonyms of the words in bold. Make any other changes necessary. There may be more than one possible answer.

### Example

*One cause of increased sleep disturbance may be that modern cities are not as **quiet** as they used to be.*

<u>*Today's cities are noisier than in the past, which could be a factor in higher levels of sleep disturbance.*</u>

**1** People also tend not to sleep for as **long** as they did fifty years ago.

**2** However, people who are unemployed seem to sleep slightly **fewer** hours than those who work at least eight hours per day.

**3** Another factor could be the increase in the number of stimulants consumed by the average person, which is far **greater** than it was.

**4** In addition, many caffeinated drinks are now **stronger** than they used to be.

### Using commas to improve the clarity of your writing

**5g** Add commas to the sentences below where necessary.

### Example

The most commonly reported causes of sleep disturbance are work worries or distractions such as TV the Internet and financial concerns.

*The most commonly reported causes of sleep disturbance are work worries, or distractions such as TV, the Internet, and financial concerns.*

**1** Steps have been taken to provide guidelines about good sleep habits yet many members of the public still are not aware of them.

**2** The most commonly reported effects of sleeplessness are lower energy lower mood and difficulty concentrating.

**3** Work-related stress which has grown hugely in recent years is fast becoming the main reported cause of sleeplessness in the over-40 age group particularly among women.

**4** Interestingly overly long periods of sleep also appear to have negative effects on mood and performance the following day.

**5** Fortunately there is greater understanding of the negative effects of sleep deprivation on mental health and even physical condition.

# Investigating

**By the end of Part C you will be able to:**

- make efficient notes
- use discourse markers to understand abstracts
- understand written discourse markers.

## 1 Making efficient notes

**1a** You have been asked to research an essay on health and life expectancy in the UK. Work in small groups. Discuss these questions.

1 What is obesity?

2 Do you think rates of obesity are currently increasing or decreasing in the UK? Why?

3 Can you think of any ways to reduce rates of obesity in the population?

**1b** As part of your research you have found this extract from a local authority report on diet and health. Read the extract. Does it confirm your ideas in 1a?

---

### Diet, eating habits and health in the UK

Having previously been somewhat overlooked, eating habits and their effect on health in the UK have more recently received greater attention in the media, and many non-experts have considered this to mean that overall the healthiness of the UK diet is improving. In fact, recent statistics suggest that public awareness of healthy eating is falling and that many people now exist on diets which provide either insufficient nutrition or contain dangerously high levels of fats, sugars and salts. According to our findings, this has a significant impact on public health: rates of obesity have risen steadily since the mid-1980s, and obesity is becoming increasingly common in young children. Figures from the NHS Health and Social Care Information Centre in 2010 suggest that in the age group 2–10 years old, around 14% of children are now classed as obese.

---

**1c** Work in pairs. Compare these notes made by a student with the original source in 1b. Underline places where you feel the notes are not effective and suggest ways of making them more efficient.

---

Source:

Eating habits + their effect previously overlooked but recently received greater attention in media. Non-experts – diet is improving. In fact, stats suggest that pub. awareness is falling and many people now on a diet have insufficient nutrition, v. high levels fats, sugars + salts.

---

One way to make your notes more efficient is to think about which words in the original text carry meaning – content words – and which are simply performing a grammatical function – function words.

**1d** Work in pairs. Look at another student's notes below and her underlining on the original source. Answer these questions.

    **1** Has the student mostly underlined content words or function words?

    **2** Has the student mostly used content words or function words in her notes?

    **3** There are 138 words in the original text. How many words are there in the student's notes?

## Diet, eating habits and health in the UK

Having previously been somewhat <u>overlooked</u>, <u>eating habits</u> and their effect on health in the UK have more <u>recently</u> received greater attention in the <u>media</u>, and many <u>non-experts</u> have <u>considered</u> this to mean that overall the <u>healthiness</u> of the UK diet is <u>improving</u>. In fact, <u>recent statistics</u> suggest that <u>public awareness of healthy eating</u> is <u>falling</u> and that <u>many people now exist on diets which provide either</u> insufficient nutrition, or contain <u>dangerously high levels of fats, sugars and salts</u>. According to our findings, this has a significant impact on public health: <u>rates of obesity</u> have risen steadily since the <u>mid-1980s</u>, and obesity is becoming <u>increasingly common in young children</u>. Figures from the <u>NHS Health and Social Care Information Centre</u> in 2010 suggest that in the <u>age group 2–10</u> years old, around <u>14% of children</u> are now classed as obese.

Notes

Healthy eating covered by media lately – popular assumption:

UK diet = improving

NOT TRUE! Recent figs: public less and less aware of healthy eating

Nutritional value of food = falling /

obesity rates = rising fr. mid-80s

2010 figs: children 2–10 yrs old – 14% obese.

---

Notes can usually be dramatically shortened by eliminating many function words (e.g. articles, prepositions, etc.).

This should not affect the quality of the information. Some function words may still be needed to maintain meaning.

---

**1e** Look at the notes in 1d. Why is the preposition *by* included after *covered*?

**1f**  Read another extract from the report. Are any of the solutions the same as you suggested in 1a? Are any different solutions mentioned?

> Several possible measures to reverse this trend towards unhealthy diet and obesity have been suggested. It seems that awareness-raising among schoolchildren is a vital step to take. Some local councils have recently approved funding for an informative theatre production to be run in schools and colleges, hoping to communicate the importance of healthy eating to children. A series of television advertisements was suggested and taken forward to the national government. In addition, a number of healthy-eating virtual information centres and websites have been established. Furthermore, it is suggested that healthy-eating campaigns be linked to similar campaigns promoting exercise, as diet-related ill health is made worse by lack of exercise. It is likely that successfully increasing the amount of time that all age groups within the population spend exercising will help to reduce obesity levels significantly.

**1g**  Underline the content words in the text in 1f which communicate the key points. You may need to underline function words you think are necessary to preserve meaning too.

**1h**  Compare your answers in small groups. Try to agree on which words are important in communicating the text's key points.

**1i**  Work in small groups. Write notes in the table using the words you underlined. Remember to use symbols and abbreviations. Try to reproduce the key ideas from the original text much more briefly by focusing on content words. Use a maximum of 50 words.

| Notes |
| --- |
|  |

## 2  Using discourse markers to understand abstracts

**2a**  You are going to look at an example abstract from an article about health when travelling abroad. Work in pairs. Discuss what steps people can take to ensure they remain in good health when in another country:

- before they go
- while they are abroad
- when they return home.

> An **abstract** is a short summary of a piece of academic research, often only about 200 words long, usually found before the introduction in an academic research journal article or dissertation. Many abstracts are structured in a similar way, so understanding *how* they are structured can help you find information more efficiently when you are looking for sources for your own academic work.

**2b** Read the information about abstracts on p.184. Work with another student and discuss:

- what the main purpose(s) of an abstract might be
- which of these areas you would expect an abstract to include information about:

*a brief introduction to the topic, a statement of a problem, a description of the methodology used to do the research, a summary of results or findings, a conclusion about what has been found (or what the findings suggest), a statement of the author's aim in writing the paper, a list of references, a list of key words*

**2c** Now read the abstract and match each numbered sentence with a function from 2b, noting them in the table. Some sentences can have more than one function.

[1]With a worldwide increase in the number of travellers visiting other countries, the speed with which highly infectious diseases can spread around the world has become the subject of a great deal of research. [2]However, studies on travel and health risks abroad often lack any research on traveller awareness of risk and the steps travellers take to minimize health risks. [3]Therefore, this research, recently carried out in the UK, attempts to discover tourists' awareness of the risks they face and tries to relate these to a number of factors, including family background, income, location in the UK and times travelled abroad. [4]250 people from different social groups, in different locations and with a variety of travel histories were interviewed. [5]Although the results strongly suggest that most travellers underestimate the danger of diseases spreading through air transport, it was found that there is a high degree of awareness of individual risk overall. [6]However, there were also significant variations in terms of social group and location. [7]Consequently we suggest that more needs to be done by UK health authorities in targeting education towards specific people with regard to the risks of travelling abroad.

Source: Hiller, A. (2007). Traveller impressions of disease risk: a perception analysis. *Tropical Health Journal*, 63, 159–172.

| Sentence | Function(s) |
|---|---|
| 1 | a brief introduction to the topic |
| 2 | |
| 3 | |
| 4 | |
| 5 | |
| 6 | |
| 7 | |

**2d** Work in pairs. Here is another abstract from a medical student's dissertation about the effect on patients when they are told they have cancer. Read it and identify the function(s) of each sentence, noting them in the table. Then discuss how similar this is to the abstract on p.185 with regard to the order of information given.

> [1]As the population has grown older, an increasing number of people in the UK have suffered from cancer. [2]Although levels of treatment have improved, a diagnosis of cancer remains, for many people, a traumatic and life-changing event. [3]Much cancer research has focused on the physical effects of cancer, but to date there has been little on how a diagnosis of cancer affects psychological well-being. [4]This study of three people who were recently told they had cancer attempts to address this by using an in-depth case study approach. [5]The results highlighted four major themes: negative life experiences, beliefs about the symptoms of cancer, the effects of diagnosis on personal beliefs, and the effect of society views of cancer. [6]It is thus suggested that these four areas are ones which should be actively discussed with patients both at the time and following their initial cancer diagnosis.

| Sentence | Function(s) |
|----------|-------------|
| 1 | |
| 2 | |
| 3 | |
| 4 | |
| 5 | |
| 6 | |

## 3 Understanding written discourse markers

### Discourse markers of concession/contrast

**3a** Read again the first two sentences from the abstract in 2c. Here are some of the main points which have been paraphrased. Put them in the order they are in the abstract.

_____ There is little research on how travellers perceive risks to their health.

_____ This has caused many diseases to spread quickly.

__1__ More people are visiting other countries.

_____ Researchers have studied this area quite thoroughly.

**3b** Decide what the relationship is between the two underlined parts of the extract on p.187.

**a** The second point is what is expected after the first point.

**b** The second point is a result of the first point.

**c** The second point is not what is expected after the first point.

**d** The second point is a detailed example of the first point.

What word is used to introduce the second point?

With a worldwide increase in the number of travellers visiting other countries, <u>the speed with which highly infectious diseases can spread around the world has become the subject of a great deal of research.</u> However, <u>studies on travel and health risks abroad often lack any research on traveller awareness of risk</u> and the steps travellers take to minimize health risks.

> *However* introduces an idea which is rather unexpected or surprising considering the previous sentence. It is important to note that by using *however* the writer does not disagree with the content of the first sentence. Rather, they accept or acknowledge that it is true (this is known as *concession*), but then introduce an idea which *contrasts* with the previous sentence and which they may wish to highlight more.

**3c** Identify and underline other discourse markers of concession/contrast in these sentences, taken from the research paper you read part of in 2c.

1 Many tourists accept the health insurance package their tour operator offers, though few of them read it or know what is contained in the details.

2 Some tourists were offered refunds on trips to areas with high levels of swine flu. Nonetheless, many did not cancel their travel plans.

3 Although many major airports checked passengers' temperatures before allowing them to board, several people still tried to travel with a fever.

4 Patients in different areas of the UK experience varying levels of healthcare. Nevertheless, people from nearly all areas were given exactly the same travel advice.

5 Responses from patients were very different, despite the interviews being held in exactly the same conditions.

6 The majority of people said they would travel again, even though they were at high risk of illness.

7 In spite of the danger of long-term health problems, more than 70% of those asked said they would visit a mosquito-infested area.

Now add the discourse markers you have identified to this table, depending on whether they link ideas across two different sentences or within just one sentence.

| Concession/contrast linking ideas across two different sentences | Concession/contrast linking ideas within just one sentence |
|---|---|
| Nonetheless | |

**3d** Look at these sentences, which use a discourse marker of concession/contrast in just one sentence, and underline the discourse marker.

a Many travellers claimed that they would not alter their plans, even though the government had issued a travel warning.

b Even though the government had issued a travel warning, many travellers claimed that they would not alter their plans.

The discourse marker can be placed *either*:

**a** after the comma but before the second idea, to introduce the contrast, *or*

**b** at the beginning of the sentence (before the first idea).

Discuss if there is a difference in meaning between the two sentences.

### Discourse markers of consequence/result

**3e** Read the next part of the abstract (in italics). Underline the word which links this to the part you have already read and discuss the questions below.

---

With a worldwide increase in the number of travellers visiting other countries, the speed with which highly infectious diseases can spread around the world has become the subject of a great deal of research. However, studies on travel and health risks abroad often lack any research on traveller awareness of risk and the steps travellers take to minimize health risks.

*Therefore, this research, recently carried out in the UK, attempts to discover tourists' awareness of the risks they face and tries to relate these to a number of factors, including family background, income, location in the UK and times travelled abroad.*

Source: Hiller, A. (2007). Traveller impressions of disease risk: a perception analysis. *Tropical Health Journal, 63*, 159–172.

---

**a** How is the discourse marker you have underlined used? Choose one.

- To introduce a concession/contrast to previous information.
- To introduce a detailed example added to previous information.
- To introduce a consequence/result of previous information.

**b** Identify and circle the previous information that this discourse marker relates to.

---

*Therefore* introduces new information that is a result or consequence of previous information. It can link information in the same sentence or across different sentences. When used to link information between two ideas in the same sentence, a conjunction (for example, *and*) must also be used.

*Examples*

*Many travellers in 2009 were well aware of the risk of swine flu **and therefore** carried protective masks with them.*

*Many travellers in 2009 were well aware of the risk of swine flu. **Therefore**, they carried protective masks with them.*

*Many travellers in 2009 were well aware of the risk of swine flu. They **therefore** carried protective masks with them.*

---

**3f** Several discourse markers have a similar meaning to *therefore*. Identify and underline these in the sentences below.

**1** A school party from the UK arrived in China showing signs of swine flu. They were consequently not allowed to leave their hotel during most of their visit.

**2** Travel warnings were then issued by some countries where swine flu rates were high. As a result, many tourists' travel plans were disrupted.

**3** Restrictions were placed on international travel for several months and thus many people lost money on the holidays they had already paid for.

**4** Several tourists contracted swine flu in Mexico early on. As a consequence, they were unable to return home until they had recovered.

**3g** For the sentences on p.188, indicate (with a *) other places in the sentence where the discourse marker could go, e.g.

    **1** A school party from the UK arrived in China showing signs of swine flu. *They were consequently not allowed to leave their hotel during most of their visit.

    Now do the same with sentences 2–4, but be careful!

> **LESSON TASK**   **4 Using abstracts to locate academic sources**

**4a** Obesity is a growing problem in some countries. Work in small groups and discuss these issues connected to obesity.

- Which countries are generally associated with obesity? Why do you think this is?
- Which parts of the population seem to be most at risk of obesity? Why do you think this is (think about age, social groups, occupation, lifestyle, etc.)?
- What consequences does obesity have (think about individuals, families, society as a whole)?
- How would you solve the problem of obesity? List at least six things in this table that might help to solve the problem.

| Solving the problem of obesity |
| --- |
| 1 |
| 2 |
| 3 |
| 4 |
| 5 |
| 6 |

**4b** You have been given an assessed task to write an essay with the following title:

*Outline the causes and effects of obesity in developed countries. Put forward some measures that might help solve the problem.*

While researching for this title, you find a number of abstracts for academic research articles connected to obesity and you need to evaluate which articles might be worth reading or not.

Work in pairs. Your tutor will give each of you two different abstracts to work with. Complete the following activities.

    **1** The first abstract has the information in the wrong order. Use what you know about the structure of abstracts to put the information in order.

    **2** The second abstract has gaps making it difficult to see how the information is organized. Complete the abstract using suitable discourse markers.

**4c** Tell your partner about the studies described in your two abstracts. As you listen to your partner telling you about their abstracts, make some brief notes about the study. Ask any questions to clarify your understanding.

**4d** With your partner, discuss together which of the articles are appropriate for the assignment title, and why.

# 5 Revision and extension

### Using content words to make brief notes

**5a** Select a paragraph or two from any text you are currently reading as part of your studies. Photocopy these paragraphs and underline the content words which carry the meaning of the key points. Then make brief notes using the content words you have underlined, paraphrasing where possible.

### Recognizing patterns in abstracts

**5b** Look at an abstract for an academic research article about the effect of music on health. Using the information in 2b, identify the function(s) of each sentence (a–h) and then put them in order (1–8) using the discourse markers to help you.

| | |
|---|---|
| a | 11 men and 13 women aged between 30 and 60, all with long-term illnesses, were given music CDs and programmes of related exercise to complete. |
| b | Music has long been used by therapists to promote healthy behaviour, especially in the area of mental health. |
| c | As a consequence, we put forward a call for health promotion and rehabilitation programmes to include music as a key feature, both at an individual level and within local communities. |
| d | From the resulting interviews, it was found that music can be a motivating influence for moving our bodies, releasing anger, and can even overcome pain. |
| e | However, there has been little research into the role and significance of music for people with long-term illnesses, especially with regard to how music might help people learn more about themselves and their illness, and in the area of rehabilitation. |
| f | However, personal taste in music was a key factor in patients' responses and completion of the exercise programme. |
| g | Consequently, this research set out to explore the role of music in supporting health, using a mixture of action-research and case study ethnography. |
| h | The study appeared to give an increase in self-awareness, consciousness, well-being and health for the majority of the participants in the study. |

| 1 | 2 | 3 | 4 | 5 | 6 | 7 | 8 |
|---|---|---|---|---|---|---|---|
| | | | | | | | |

### Discourse markers

**5c** Complete these sentences from academic text books, using a suitable discourse marker to show concession.

1 _____ they have some knowledge of the possible effects of global warming on the environment, many adults are unaware of how it may affect their own health.

2 _____ the effects of air pollution have received a lot of media attention, the problems caused by noise pollution have recently been more widely reported.

**3** _____ the high risks of UV exposure, many Britons still do not regularly use sun cream.

**4** Cases of asthma are still increasing in cities, _____ government measures to reduce air pollution.

**5** Crops failed due to drought in some areas last summer, _____ rainfall was higher than average nationally.

**5d** Here are two short extracts from academic articles on health issues. Fill the gaps with a suitable discourse marker.

**1** International travel presents travellers with potential dangers to their health. Individuals arriving in territories with different health situations are at heightened risk of sickness if they have not received accurate medical advice about conditions in that country. _____[1], it is uncertain whether the majority of travellers seek, or act on, health advice for their destination countries. _____[2], there is a need for careful research to evaluate how well educated individuals are about staying healthy while travelling.

**2** The ease and affordability of international travel mean that increasing numbers of people visit other countries each year. This increase in travel means that many more people are now exposed to infectious diseases and other serious health risks. _____[1], the effects of illness related to travel cost the health service millions of pounds each year. _____[2], travel-related illness is not just a health problem, but an economic one also. There is a serious question, _____[3], about whether enough travellers try actively to protect their health by seeking medical advice before they travel.

### Extension: discourse markers

> *Even so* and *still* can be used in a similar way to *however, nonetheless* and *nevertheless*. They are used to join two sentences together, but are not used in all the positions that *however, nonetheless* and *nevertheless* are.

**5e** Look at these examples. Underline the discourse markers *still* and *even so* to see which position they should be used in to connect ideas.

**1** Recent summers have seen heatwaves in which people have been advised to stay indoors and drink plenty of fluids. Even so, hundreds of deaths across Europe have been attributed to the heat.

**2** Experts are seriously concerned about severe water shortages in the near future. Still, as water is so abundant now in most developed countries, few people are worried about this.

Now rewrite sentences 1–3 from 5c using *still* or *even so*.

**1**_____

**2**_____

**3**_____

**Using abstracts to assess the relevance of a text**

**5f** Photocopy (or cut, paste and print) some examples of abstracts you have found when searching for sources for an essay you are currently writing or a presentation you are currently planning as part of your studies. Follow instructions 1–3.

1 Underline the discourse markers.

2 Make notes on how the discourse markers enabled you to follow the pattern of the abstract.

3 Make notes on how this pattern helped you decide whether the abstract was relevant.

# Reporting in speech

**By the end of Part D you will be able to:**

- express the aims of a presentation using clauses of purpose
- understand differences between spoken and written academic English
- understand and use connected speech.

## 1 Expressing the aims of a presentation using clauses of purpose

> The introduction of a presentation should help the audience understand the purpose of the talk: what you are going to talk about, and why you have chosen to focus on these points. It should help them follow the presentation and recognize your position or argument.
>
> Purpose can be, and often is, expressed explicitly with phrases such as *in this presentation, we aim to ...*, *our goal today is ...* or *in this presentation, my purpose is ....* You looked at some similar ways of expressing aims in written work in Unit 1. Purpose can also be expressed in other ways.

**1a** You are going to listen to an extract from the introduction to a presentation on sleep deprivation. Before you listen, work in small groups. Discuss these questions and write notes.

1 Do you think that sleep deprivation is a serious problem? Why / why not?

2 What are the long-term health risks associated with sleep deprivation?

3 Do you think the government should carry out public awareness campaigns about good sleeping habits?

| Notes |
|-------|
| 1 |
| 2 |
| 3 |

**1b** Listen to the extract from the presentation with the title *Sleep deprivation – a widespread but hidden problem*. What does the speaker aim to show?

4.11

**1c** Listen to the extract again and write the sentence which shows the speaker's purpose.

| Purpose |
| --- |
|  |

**1d** Check your answers with a partner.

**1e** Work in pairs. Discuss these questions.

    **1** Why did the speaker use the title *A widespread but hidden problem*?
Use the sentence you wrote down in 1c to help you.

    **2** What structure in 1c does the speaker use to show they are addressing the
question *Why*?

      **a** *-ing* form
      **b** an expression (e.g. *our goal is*)
      **c** *to*-infinitive

> You can use the *to*-infinitive to show purpose (or answer the question *Why?*).
> The infinitive is followed by a clause which explains the purpose.
>
> ***Example***
> *We are presenting this information to show <u>the need for healthcare reform</u>*
> *<u>across the UK</u>.*

**1f** Work in pairs. Match the beginnings and endings of these extracts from three
presentations about sleep disturbance.

| | |
| --- | --- |
| **1** Today's presentation discusses the role of lifestyle in sleep problems | **a** to demonstrate that sleeping well is not only important for day-to-day functioning, but also for long-term health. |
| **2** The short-term effects of sleep deprivation are well known, but how serious are the long-term effects? We focus on these | **b** to determine to what extent your habits while awake can impact your ability to get a good night's sleep. |
| **3** In this presentation I will explore the effect of caffeine intake on sleep patterns | **c** to show that increasing consumption of caffeinated drinks is having a serious impact on the nation's health. |

**1g** Listen and check your answers.

4.12

**1h** Listen to two extracts from presentations on the importance of sleep. For each
extract, decide who the audience is.

4.13

    **a** A group of parents
    **b** A group of teenagers
    **c** A group of university lecturers
    **d** A group of nurses

**1i** Listen again. Decide what the purpose of each presentation (a or b) is.

**1** The aim of presentation 1 is
  **a** to show parents how to help their children develop sensible sleeping habits.
  **b** to persuade parents that their children should be sleeping more.

**2** The aim of presentation 2 is
  **a** to offer a group of nurses further training about helping insomnia sufferers.
  **b** to criticize a group of nurses for failure to treat insomnia sufferers properly.

**1j** Listen again. Match these phrases with the presentation in which you hear them.

  **a** so as to _____

  **b** in order to _____

---

These phrases introduce clauses of purpose. They frequently appear in *to-infinitive* clauses.

### Examples
*Today's presentation discusses the role of lifestyle in sleep problems **so as to** determine to what extent your habits while awake can impact your ability to get a good night's sleep.*

*In this presentation I will explore the effect of caffeine intake on sleep patterns **in order to** show that increasing consumption of caffeinated drinks is having a serious impact on the nation's health.*

---

**1k** Choose four presentation topics on the subject *Teenagers and health* from the list below. For each topic, write a sentence for the introduction to show the purpose of your presentation.

Use this structure as a model:

*In today's presentation on* [topic of presentation, selected from the list below], *I will focus on* [specific focus of presentation] [show your purpose by using a clause of purpose starting with an infinitive].

### Example
*In today's presentation on teenage sleeping habits, I will focus on the use of a routine of set sleeping times as a way to overcome insomnia, in order to investigate how effective this method is compared to other insomnia treatments.*

| | |
|---|---|
| government enforcement of health laws | smoking |
| health challenges when living away from home | sports facilities available to teenagers |
| | teenage sleeping habits |
| parents' influence over teenagers' health | teenagers and diet |
| peers' influence over teenagers' health | the school curriculum and teenagers' health |
| physical exercise | |

1

2

3

4

## 2 Understanding differences between spoken and written academic English

> The content of an academic presentation may often be the same as in a written report or essay. However, in a presentation the speaker may demonstrate features of spoken language which are not suitable in a formal written context.

**2a** Work in pairs. Decide whether these features of language (1–8) are features of spoken (S) or written (W) academic language, or both (B).

1 quantifiers such as *lots of, a little* _____

2 quantifiers such as *a great deal* _____

3 personal pronouns such as *he, she, they* _____

4 personal pronouns such as *I, we, you* _____

5 rhetorical questions _____

6 contractions (e.g. *won't, didn't, I'm*) _____

7 non-defining relative clauses _____

8 short sentences _____

**2b** You are going to listen to another extract from the presentation with the title *Sleep deprivation – a widespread but hidden problem.* Work in pairs. Before you listen, discuss this question and write notes.

| How does poor sleep make people feel in the short term? |
| --- |
|  |

4.14

**2c** Listen to the extract. Were the ideas in the extract the same as yours in 2b?

**2d** Listen again. Which of the language features in 2a did you hear?

> Presentation speakers often use the personal pronouns *you* and *we* to include the audience and make them engage with the presentation. However, generalizations such as *we are all aware* can be inappropriate if there is no shared knowledge. It is important, therefore, to know your audience and to refer to them and their knowledge appropriately.

**2e** Look at the extracts on p.197 from written texts on teenage health. Choose the correct summary (a or b) for each extract.

**Extract 1**

> Contemporary teenagers tend to be under more pressure to study hard and may find it more difficult to find time for relaxation or exercise.

a Teenagers usually find it very difficult to find time to relax or exercise, due to pressure to get good results at school.

b Parents are usually understanding of their children and do not put pressure on them to study hard.

**Extract 2**

> Freshers' week (the first week of term for new university students) is traditionally a time for parties and events which encourage new students to make friends and participate in sports, clubs, and the social life of the university. This makes Freshers' week an ideal time to promote regular exercise and healthy activities. Consequently, a calendar of sports- and exercise-related events is now offered in many student unions. In others, guidelines have been produced which require university societies and departments to offer a variety of activities in the first weeks of term. These may range from traditional social events, such as welcome parties, to more cultural or sporting events, such as visits to local places of interest or local walks.

a Many student unions make it compulsory to participate in exercise and sports clubs in the first weeks of term.

b Many student unions ensure that the first week's activities include sports and promote a range of healthy activities.

**Extract 3**

> Over the last thirty years, the way children and young people spend their leisure time has changed dramatically. For a long time it was the norm for young people to spend the majority of their free time outside the home, playing outdoor games or sports. However, in recent years what has changed almost beyond recognition is how young teenagers use their leisure time. It is now quite common for young children and teenagers to spend the majority of their time inside the family home, pursuing indoor leisure activities such as playing computer games or using the Internet. However, despite this massive change in behaviour patterns, members of older generations still tend to believe that childhood should be spent playing outdoors.

a Leisure habits in the UK haven't changed for decades, and members of all generations enjoy outdoor activities.

b Leisure habits in the UK have changed in recent decades, meaning that members of older generations often have an idea of childhood which does not match the current reality.

2f Check your answers with a partner.

2g Work in pairs. Prepare a spoken presentation of one of the written extracts in 2e for an audience of students from your course. Try to rephrase the information in the extract using personal pronouns in a way that is appropriate to the audience.

**2h** Look at these extracts from the lecture *Sleep deprivation – a widespread but hidden problem*. Check any words that you don't understand in a dictionary. Then, work in pairs. Decide if the language is more formal (F) or more informal (I).

1 Today's presentation is **titled** ... ＿＿＿

2 First, **though**, ... ＿＿＿

3 a **broad overview** of (problem) ＿＿＿

4 **around** 60% of us ＿＿＿

5 to **address** the problem ＿＿＿

6 **high-profile** disasters ＿＿＿

7 as you **just** mentioned ＿＿＿

8 it is therefore **imperative** ＿＿＿

9 provide appropriate **support** ＿＿＿

10 We live in a **24/7** world ＿＿＿

11 we have a **tough job** ＿＿＿

> In academic spoken texts such as lectures or oral presentations there is likely to be a mix of more formal and more informal language. Speakers in academic situations are likely to use more formal or technical vocabulary to describe key information, but use more informal conversational language elsewhere.

**2i** Complete this table using the words and phrases in bold in 2h.

| More formal | More informal |
| --- | --- |
| high-profile | well-known |
| approximately | |
| | big picture |
| constantly busy | |
| | help |
| difficult | |
| | named |
| however | |
| | talk about |
| previously | |
| task | |
| | very important |

**2j** Work in small groups. Discuss these questions and write notes in the table below.

1 For those words where you don't already know a synonym with a different level of formality, where can you find synonyms and information on levels of formality?

2 How could you incorporate this information into your personal vocabulary logbook?

| Notes |
| --- |
| |

**2k** How do you think the language of a presentation's visual aids (for example, PowerPoint slides or a poster) might differ from the spoken part of the presentation?

**2l** Practise using this more formal/informal vocabulary by being formal/informal interpreters. Work in teams. Your teacher will read you a sentence using one of the words from the list in 2i. Rephrase that sentence into its formal/informal equivalent. When your team thinks you have rephrased correctly, alert your teacher and read your sentence. The first team to rephrase correctly wins a point!

## 3 Understanding and using connected speech

**3a** Practise saying these sentences aloud, at a natural speed. What happens to the pronunciation of the 't' or 'd' sounds at the end of the first word in each underlined pair?

    **1** We're now going to look <u>at these</u> problems in the <u>short term</u>.

    **2** As it's been pointed out at <u>least twice</u>, the <u>hard disk</u> needs replacing.

    **3** The Prime Minister should have <u>kept talking at this</u> point.

4.15

**3b** Listen to the sentences. Make a note of how the speakers pronounce the underlined words.

**3c** Compare your answers with a partner. Discuss what kinds of sounds:

- disappear
- follow the sounds that disappear.

> In spoken English, the boundaries between words are often ignored, so that the end of one word and the beginning of the next merge together. This is known as *connected speech*. In connected speech, some sounds may disappear, either between words or within one word.

**3d** Work in pairs. Try to predict which sounds will disappear in connected speech in these sentences.

    **1** One significant factor the researchers seemed not to notice was the lack of transport. (3 sounds)

    **2** The one thing that would have helped to combat this problem was missing. (2 sounds)

    **3** There is a great deal of evidence to suggest that the lab passed the test on, but kept quiet about the results. (7 sounds)

4.16

**3e** Listen and check your answers. Then practise saying the sentences aloud.

**3f** Work in pairs. Make a note of the rules for disappearing sounds in the space below.

| Disappearing sound | Position | Following letter |
|---|---|---|
| /t/ | | |
| /d/ | | |

> As well as sounds being dropped in connected speech, sometimes extra sounds are added. This happens most often between words which end and begin with vowel sounds. The most common added sounds are /w/, /j/ and /r/.

**4.17**

**3g** Listen to these extracts from the presentation on *Sleep deprivation – a widespread but hidden problem*, first as individual words, then as connected speech. Write the extra sounds /w/, /j/ or /r/ above the place they are added in connected speech.

   1 Hello, and thank you all for coming.

   2 Some of the effects are harmful.

   3 There is a great deal of evidence for this.

**3h** Work in pairs. Discuss when extra sounds might be added in connected speech.

**3i** Listen again and practise saying the sentences in 3g aloud.

**3j** Work in pairs. Try to predict where and which sounds will be added to these sentences in connected speech.

   1 I would like to introduce my colleague, who is a researcher. (2 sounds)

   2 We are all aware of the short-term effects. (2 sounds)

   3 Sleep deprivation is also a significant factor in road accidents. (2 sounds)

   4 The issue of poor sleep is apparently unnoticed. (3 sounds)

   5 There are a number of national projects which will go ahead soon. (4 sounds)

**4.18**

**3k** Listen and check your answers. Write the extra sounds /w/, /j/ or /r/ above the places they are added in connected speech. Then practise saying the sentences aloud.

---

> **LESSON TASK**    **4 Introducing a presentation**

**4a** You are going to prepare and present the introduction to a short talk on a health issue affecting teenagers. The introduction should last about two minutes. Work in pairs. Choose a topic from 1k. You don't need to have a lot of knowledge about the topic.

**4b** Work in pairs. Plan your introduction and make some notes to help you plan what to say. In particular, think about:
   • how you will express the purpose of your talk
   • the level of formality of the language you will use
   • how you will use features of connected speech.

**4c** Work in groups of four. Take turns to present your introduction to the other pair in your group. As you listen, write examples of the language you hear in this table.

| Expressing purpose | Formality |
| --- | --- |
|  |  |

**4d** Compare the examples of language you wrote in the table in 4c with the other students' plan. Did they include all the language they intended to? Did they include examples of all the language points in this Part?

## 5 Review and extension

### Clauses of purpose: alternatives to *so as to* and *in order to*

**5a** Rewrite your sentences from 1k, using *so that* and *in order that*.

> Presentation 1
>
> Presentation 2
>
> Presentation 3

4.19

**5b** Listen and complete these extracts from presentations on sleep deprivation using phrases which mean *so as to* or *in order to*.

1 We have used this title _____
   highlight the fact …

2 Today I'll talk to you about two cases I dealt with last year _____
   _____ you recognize that …

3 … particularly in teenagers, _____
   are better prepared …

### Clauses of purpose

> In informal English, the *that* may be dropped from *so that*, showing purpose with *so* alone.
>
> Compare these sentences.
>
> *Today's presentation aims to examine the latest findings from sleep research, so that you can help patients to improve the quality of their sleep.*
>
> *I wanted to talk to you today about how we understand the latest research about sleep habits, so we can help our patients to improve the quality of their sleep.*

### Negative clauses of purpose

4.20

**5c** Listen to some extracts from presentations on the importance of teenagers' diets. Complete the extracts with the words or phrases that you hear.

1 I am going to talk to you today about the importance of eating healthily in front of your teenage children, _____ _____ _____ _____ transmit any negative relationship you have with food to them.

2 This presentation discusses the importance of including normal and plus-size models in teen magazines, _____ _____ they _____ _____ encourage conditions such as anorexia nervosa.

3 Today's presentation will outline two success stories _____ _____ _____ you _____ _____ see healthy products as unmarketable to teenagers.

**4** We support the ban on advertising fast food, _____ _____ _____ _____ give teenagers the message that consuming such products is healthy or desirable.

**5** It's important that unhealthy dietary habits are still allowed, _____ teenagers _____ _____ rebel against what they might consider strict rules.

**6** Our aim today is _____ _____ _____ on the negative consequences of a poor diet, _____ _____ _____ at the positive results of eating healthily.

**5d** Complete these rules about negative clauses of purpose.

**1** With *in order to* and *so as to*, the word _____ comes before *to* + infinitive.

**2** With *so that*, *in order that*, and *so*, the negative clause of purpose is formed by subject + negative _____ verb.

**5e** Complete these sentences using either a positive or negative clause of purpose, using the information in brackets to help you.

**1** Today's presentation suggests some alternative methods that people suffering sleep problems could try _____
(help them get a better night's sleep).

**2** This presentation discusses the responsibility student leisure facilities have to maintain more traditional opening hours _____
(not encourage students to disrupt their study routine by staying up late).

**3** We discuss the measures school canteens can take _____
_____ (not make a healthy diet more expensive than fast food options).

**4** We show how adult smokers' stories can be positively used _____
_____ (help teenagers resist or quit the habit).

**5** In this presentation ideas for better leisure facilities for teenagers in this town are proposed, _____ (provide constructive pastimes and encourage sports and exercise).

### Understanding some of the differences between written and spoken English

> Students are frequently asked to give an oral presentation based on a written paper. It is never a good idea to simply read your paper aloud as a presentation.

**5f** Choose one or two points (one or two paragraphs of written text should be enough) from an academic text you have written in the past and consider how you could present the same information orally. Do not script a whole presentation but think about the language you will use.

# Reporting in writing

**By the end of Part E you will be able to:**

- show your position using adverbs and adjectives
- make recommendations and give warnings in conclusions
- develop your writing style by varying the length of sentences.

## 1 Showing your position using adverbs and adjectives

**1a** Work in pairs. Which adverbs in the box show a stronger opinion (S) and which show more caution (C)? Write notes below.

| apparently | arguably | clearly | crucially | especially |
| naturally | obviously | possibly | potentially | presumably |
| | undeniably | undoubtedly | unquestionably | |

| Adverbs of comment |
| --- |
| undeniably (S) |

**1b** You are going to read an extract from the conclusion to an essay about alternative health remedies. Work in pairs. Discuss these questions.

**1** What are alternative health remedies? Have you ever tried one?

**2** How effective do you think alternative remedies are compared to modern medicine?

**1c** Read this extract from a conclusion to a student essay and answer these questions.

**1** What was the aim of the essay?

**2** Did the writer's research find alternative remedies to be successful?

**3** Did the writer's research find alternative remedies to be safe?

> This paper has attempted to examine how effective alternative remedies are for treating minor illnesses. <u>It is undeniable that patients taking these remedies found some success</u> in alleviating both the symptoms and the duration of diseases such as the common cold. However, serious doubts were raised both over the dosage and of the risks of combining some remedies with other medication.

**1d** Read the extract again and answer these questions about the underlined phrase.

    **1** What expression with an adjective does the writer use to comment on the general results of the research?

    **2** What comment adverb could you use to replace it?

**1e** You are going to read an extract from the introduction to an essay about the health issues surrounding fossil fuels. Work in pairs. Discuss these questions.

    **1** How safe or dangerous are fossil fuels?

    **2** What specific health risks are associated with coal-fired power stations?

**1f** Read the extract. What is the writer's attitude towards the safety of coal-fired power stations in terms of our health? Underline any phrases with adjectives that the writer uses to comment on the health risks. The first one has been done for you.

> Coal-fired power stations are widely used to generate electricity for homes and industry in Western Europe, but fossil fuels are commonly regarded as one of the dirtiest forms of energy. However, it is difficult to establish whether there are any significant health risks posed to those who live near coal-fired power stations. There is some evidence of higher instances of serious disease in areas around coal-fired power stations, but it is not clear if this is a physical or psychological effect. It is necessary, therefore, to investigate the issue from different perspectives.

**1g** Read the extract in 1f again and answer these questions about the underlined parts.

    **1** Which adjectives are used to show comment?

    **2** What subject and verb are used with these adjectives?

    **3** What verb form follows the adjectives?

    **4** If the first part of the phrases, including the adjectives of comment, were removed, would the sentences still make sense?

**1h** Work in small groups. Brainstorm other adjectives which a writer can use to show their position. Write them in this box.

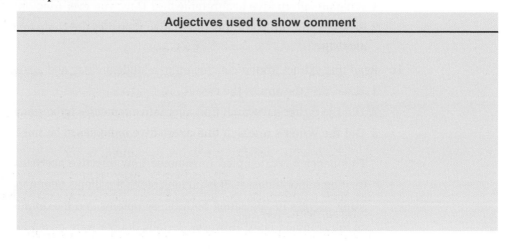

**Adjectives used to show comment**

**1i** Work in pairs. Decide which of the adjectives in 1h can be used in these forms.

   **1** *it is ... that*

   **2** *it is ... to*

   **3** both of the above.

**1j** Briefly discuss your position on the risks to health of burning fossil fuels using some of the adjectives in 1h.

   ***Examples***
   * It is *important* (that/to) ...
   * It is *doubtful* (that) ...
   * It is *interesting* (that/to) ... , etc.

## 2 Making recommendations and giving warnings in conclusions

> In essays or dissertations, the conclusion often contains a *call for action* in order to address some of the unresolved issues presented in the written paper. A call for action can be directed at a general reader or a more specific audience. It can suggest further research, or more practical steps that could be taken to resolve an issue. Calls for action often include warnings, to show what might happen if no action is taken.

**2a** You are going to read the conclusion to an essay about the health risks connected with chemicals in food production. Work in pairs. Discuss these questions.

   **1** Why are chemicals used in the production of food?

   **2** Is there any need to worry about the chemicals in your food? Why / why not?

**2b** Read the conclusion and check your answers.

> The use of chemicals in food production has boomed in recent decades, helping to produce far greater quantities of durable, resistant food for a growing population. However, research into the effect these chemicals have on our health has already suggested worrying links to some cancers and other life-changing conditions. If we continue to consume foods whose growth and preparation has involved chemicals, it is likely that far more damage to our health will be caused.

**2c** Read the conclusion again and answer these questions.

   **1** What condition and consequence does the writer raise in the last sentence? Underline the condition and circle the consequence.

   **2** What word is used to introduce the condition?

   **3** What tense is used in the condition clause? (ignore the *whose* clause)

   **4** Which phrase in the consequence clause shows the writer's level of certainty of the consequence?

   **5** Which tense does the writer use for the consequence itself?

> The structure *if* + present tense (condition), future tense (consequence) is often used in conclusions. It shows what will happen in the future as a consequence of a present action or state.
>
> The condition clause can come before the consequence clause or it is possible to reverse the order of the clauses, e.g. *If we continue to consume chemically produced foods, more damage to our health will be caused.*
>
> OR
>
> *More damage to our health will be caused if we continue to consume chemically produced foods.*
>
> However, an academic writer is also likely to show their level of certainty of the consequence using phrases such as: *it is likely / it is probable / it is quite possible*, etc. or by using a different modal from *will*, e.g. *If we continue to consume chemically produced foods, more damage to our health may/could be caused.*

**2d**  There are other ways writers may express these conditions and consequences. Complete these sentences (1–4) with the correct words from this list. There may be more than one possible answer.

| As long as | If … not | Provided that | Unless |
| --- | --- | --- | --- |

1  _____ we do _____ reduce the use of these chemicals in food production, it is likely that far more damage to our health will be caused.

2  _____ we continue to consume foods whose growth and preparation has involved chemicals, it is likely that far more damage to our health will be caused.

3  _____ we reduce the use of these chemicals in food production, it is likely that far more damage to our health will be caused.

4  _____ we reduce the use of these chemicals in food production, it is likely that we can limit damage to our health.

**2e**  Check your answers with a partner and discuss any differences in meaning between the words in the list.

**2f**  Work in pairs. Correct the errors in these sentences.

1 Unless governments will make laws to limit carbon emissions, many industries will continue to pollute.

2 It will be difficult to reduce stress for many employees if companies will not strictly limit working hours.

**2g**  Work in small groups. Think of five recommendations about essay writing. Write notes in the table on p.207. Think about:

1 planning your essay

2 searching for information

3 using other writers' ideas

4 writing the body paragraphs

5 using academic language.

| Condition | Consequence |
| --- | --- |
| you plan your essay carefully | you will find it easier to organize your paragraphs |
| 1 | |
| 2 | |
| 3 | |
| 4 | |
| 5 | |

**2h** Write sentences using your notes in 2g. Use *if (not) / provided that / as long as / unless*.

1

2

3

4

5

## 3   Developing your writing style by varying the length of sentences

**3a**   You are going to look at three extracts from students' essays about smoking in public places. Work in pairs and discuss these questions.

1   Do you think smoking in public places is dangerous? Why / why not?

2   Do you support a ban on smoking in public places? Why / why not?

**3b**   Read extract 1 below. Does the writer believe a ban on smoking is necessary?

**1**

> Smoking is often seen as unhealthy. It can affect a smoker's health. It can also affect the health of those around them. However, the negative effects of smoking may be exaggerated. The potential problems can be eliminated. The purpose of this paper is to analyze the implications of banning smoking in public places. This paper argues that valid reasons can be found to justify allowing smoking in public places.

**2**

> Although smoking is often seen as unhealthy and can affect not only a smoker's health but also the health of those around them, the negative effects of smoking may be exaggerated. The purpose of this paper is to show that the potential problems can be limited by analyzing the implications of banning smoking in public places in order to show that valid reasons can be found to justify allowing smoking in public places.

**3**

> Smoking is often seen as unhealthy. It can affect not only a smoker's health but also that of those around them. However, the negative effects of smoking may be exaggerated, as the potential problems can be eliminated. The purpose of this paper is to analyze the implications of banning smoking in public places. It argues that valid reasons can be found to justify allowing smoking in public.

**3c**   Read extracts 1–3 and answer these questions.

1   Which text has the longest sentences?

2   Which text has a variety of sentence lengths?

3   Which text is most effective at getting its message across?

The clarity and tone of a text are affected by sentence length.

Short, simple sentences can help keep your writing clear. However, too many short sentences together can make your reader feel uncomfortable (e.g. extract 1).

Long sentences can help you connect ideas together. However, be careful to avoid repetition and unnecessary words. In addition, it can be difficult to follow very long sentences, or many long sentences together.

It is preferable to include a variety of long and short sentences.

**3d** Work in small groups. Discuss these questions and write notes in this table.

1 What structures could you use to join shorter sentences together?

2 What structures could you use to divide longer sentences?

| Structures for combining shorter sentences | Structures for dividing longer sentences |
|---|---|
| relative clauses | discourse markers, e.g. *however* |

**3e** You are going to read an extract from the introduction to an essay about stress at work. Work in pairs and discuss these questions.

1 What factors may lead to stress at work?

2 What are some of the negative effects of stress in the workplace?

**3f** Read the extract. Check your answers to 3e with a partner.

Many recent studies have highlighted the growing incidence of stress at work. Employees generally now work 20% longer than their parents' generation. Their duties at work are also typically much more varied. As such, they are expected to perform expertly in a number of areas. These may range from social networking to IT to oral presentations. In addition, travelling times to and from work have increased. This is because people often now live further from their place of work. As a result of their lifestyles, workers may become so stressed that they are told to take sick leave by their doctors. Companies' productivity therefore decreases and money is lost. However, employers seem to do little to reduce staff workloads. This study aims to investigate the reason why employees are pushed to work so hard ...

**3g** Work in pairs. Try to improve the extract in 3f by joining together some of the shorter sentences.

## 4 Reviewing proofreading skills

> Proofreading – checking and revising your written work – is an essential stage in the writing process.

**4a** Work in small groups. Do you agree with these statements about proofreading? Why / why not?

1 Proofreading should be done all the way through the writing process, not just at the final draft.

2 Proofreading your own work is a waste of time because you can never see your own mistakes.

3 Proofreading another student's work and making corrections is not allowed, as it becomes no longer their original work.

4 It is a good idea to ask a student of a different nationality/language from you to do your proofreading.

5 The best person to proofread your written work is your tutor – they'll be happy to help you with this.

**4b** Work in pairs. Proofread the first draft of another student's essay. Write comments and corrections on the essay.

### Evaluate the factors which can contribute to low health expectancy in developed countries.

Throughout the ages, human health has been a topic of concern. Nowadays, with technology developed, the level of human life also gradually increasing. people can live in the better life, but can people live healthy? In developed countries, such as the United Kingdom, hough their life better than developing countries, the developed world also have a problem that is poor. On the one hand, as technology has developed more and more, that some factors about environment such as air pollution, thus affecting people's health. On the other hand, because of social competition and pressure of work now people are likely to suffer from mental or psychological illness. In addition, life style is important like people who like smoking or drinking that is bad for health. These may also be caused the body's disease. In this eaasy, first I will argue that how the enviromnent affect people's health in the UK and USA. Second I will argue how the mental health affects British and American health. Thirdly, I will argue that the factor that is life style including smoking and drinking which can contribute to low health expectancy in the UK and USA. The next proposal is to promote comprehensive measures of population health such as protect the environment, read more books for self-regulation that can reduce mental and psychological burden. At the last, healthy life style can increase the body's resistance so as to promote physical health.

The first point, the human living environment more or less affect human health. Since the industrial revolution, burning of fossil fuels such as coal, oil, increases the amount of harmful gases, polluted air. Humans can breathe these gases by the body to a certain extent of damage (Enviromnental Protection Agency, 2008) for example, vehicle emissions, factory chemicals, dust and so on,. The air is polluted. Some air pollutants, such as smoke, is toxic. Inhaled they affect health. Likely to suffer from heart or lung disease. Air pollution, elderly and children were more likely to cause disease. Larry (2005) argue that the majority of American people live in unsafe level areas, either smog or particle pollution. 76.5 million Americans survive in areas where there are unhealthy short-run levels of particle pollution. Children and the elderly are particularly at risk.

Short-run or acute, exposure to particle pollution has been linked to increases in a lot of disease such as heart attacks, strokes, emergency-room visits for asthma and cardiovascular diseases in the UK. (Bridges, 2010) reported that during the 2003 heatwave in New York, 21–38% of the deaths are due to excessive air pollution. In towns and cities, 70% of the pollution is caused by the transport, it links to the majority of health problems.

**4c** Work in groups of four. Compare and discuss:

- any mistakes you found
- how you marked mistakes and corrections on the essay draft
- how you carried out the process of proofreading. For example, how many times did you read the essay? Did you try to find every mistake? Why / why not?

**4d** Work in pairs. Discuss the advantages and disadvantages of these strategies.

1 Proofread the whole text, stopping to correct each language point as you go along.
2 Proofread the text, section by section, checking all language features in each section.
3 Proofread the text once for overall cohesion, and then again, section by section, for language points.
4 Group the language points together (e.g. all punctuation, all vocabulary, all cohesion, etc.) and proofread the text once for each group.

## 5  Review and extension

### Showing your position: using adjectives

**5a** Consider your position carefully in an essay you have written. How clearly is your position expressed in your introduction and conclusion? Rewrite the introduction and conclusion to include some examples of comment adverbs and *it is* + adjective + *to/that* ... structures.

### Making your writing more interesting: varying sentence lengths

**5b** Check an essay you have written to see how much variety in sentence length there is in each paragraph. If paragraphs are mostly comprised of very short sentences, try to make some of them longer. If paragraphs are mostly comprised of very long sentences (or contain one very long sentence), try to divide some of these into shorter sentences.

# Appendices

## Appendix 1

### Transcript of a talk on strategies for learning vocabulary

As a student studying in a language which is not your native language, you will constantly be coming across words with which you are unfamiliar. It is crucial, therefore, that you formulate a strategy for learning these new words and steadily increase your knowledge of the vocabulary which you are most likely to encounter in your studies or research. The exact methods you use to achieve this can vary from one individual to another. However, there are a few basic questions which you should consider while you design your strategy. Perhaps at their most basic, these four questions might be:

1 What words do you want to **focus** on?

2 What exactly do you mean by 'a word'?

3 What exactly do you mean by 'learn' a word?

4 What are the best ways to 'learn' the vocabulary items you have targeted?

So, firstly, what words do you want to focus on? Clearly, there are groups of words which are used in an academic **context** more frequently than non-academic contexts and these should be your main concern at this stage. There are published guides or lists of 'academic' words which you might want to do some research on. There are also some very good books to help you learn these words in specific contexts. You might want to work your way through one or more of these. Whether you do this or not, it is important that you start to develop your own record of words you feel are important in your own academic context. Perhaps you could make separate lists for words you feel you are likely to come across in a general academic context, and those you feel are more **specific** to your own **discipline** or are more technical in nature. You might also try to place the words into different **categories**, according to how or where they are most likely to be used. You should be refining these categories constantly as your records increase.

Of course, to be able to do this properly, you must first decide what you mean by 'a word'. You should always consider the different forms in a word family and group these together. For example, if you come across the word *analyze*, you need to explore what other forms of the word might be used in different contexts – words such as *analysis*, *analytical* or *analytically* and even *analyst*. You should make sure you are familiar with them all and can use them all correctly. You will sometimes find that the same word can be used for different **purposes**; for example, *lecture* can be used as a noun and as a verb. And this brings us on to the question of what you mean by 'learn' a word. It is not enough to just learn how to use a word in one context; you need to think about how that word is used in different ways. You should also think about how the pronunciation of a word might change depending on how it is being used. For example, the word *project*, when used as a noun, is pronounced differently from when it is used as a verb, due to changing syllable stress. So it might be helpful to record the pronunciation as well as the spelling and meaning of the word.

So, finally, what are the best ways to learn the vocabulary you record? To some extent, these are decided by personal preference guided, perhaps, by recommendations made either by your tutors, or by researchers or by other students who have found a certain approach successful. Whichever approach you use, it should certainly involve using the vocabulary and using it in particular contexts and for specific purposes rather than simply memorizing lists of individual words.

## Appendix 2

### Phonemic alphabet

### Vowels

#### Short vowels

| /ə/ | /æ/ | /ʊ/ | /ɒ/ | /ɪ/ | /i/ | /e/ | /ʌ/ |
|---|---|---|---|---|---|---|---|
| teacher ago | apple plan | book could | on got | in swim | happy easy | wet any | cup under |

#### Long vowels

| /ɜː/ | /ɑː/ | /uː/ | /ɔː/ | /iː/ |
|---|---|---|---|---|
| shirt learn | car mark | blue who | walk talk | eat meet |

#### Diphthongs

| /eə/ | /ɪə/ | /ʊə/ | /ɔɪ/ | /aɪ/ | /eɪ/ | /əʊ/ | /aʊ/ |
|---|---|---|---|---|---|---|---|
| chair where | near hear | tour | boy noisy | nine write | eight late | go over | brown sound |

### Consonants

#### Voiced

| /b/ | /ð/ | /v/ | /dʒ/ | /d/ | /z/ | /g/ | /ʒ/ |
|---|---|---|---|---|---|---|---|
| bit but | mother other | very live | job page | down red | magazine | girl bag | television |

| /m/ | /n/ | /ŋ/ | /l/ | /r/ | /w/ | /j/ |
|---|---|---|---|---|---|---|
| me name | now rain | thing drink | late hello | carry write | we white | you yes |

#### Unvoiced

| /p/ | /θ/ | /f/ | /tʃ/ | /t/ | /s/ | /k/ | /ʃ/ | /h/ |
|---|---|---|---|---|---|---|---|---|
| park shop | think both | face laugh | chips chair | time white | see rice | cold look | shoe fish | hot hand |

## Appendix 3

It is not surprising that diseases such as cholera, typhoid and influenza played a huge part in reducing life expectancy in the nineteenth century. **Incidentally**, did any of you read about the cholera outbreak in Peru last week? **Anyway**, although these diseases were more common amongst the poor, the rich were by no means able to escape.

## Appendix 4

In the western world today, we take the quantity and variety of food available to us for granted. However, two hundred years ago, people were only able to eat what they could provide for themselves. That is to say, they only had what they could grow, or what they could trade locally. If plant disease or poor weather meant that the food supply failed – what I mean to say is, if their crops died – people quickly became malnourished and even starved to death. This reliance on locally grown produce also meant that variety was severely limited – I mean, many people could only afford, and only had access to, a few different vegetables for much of the year. Do not forget as well that even where food was plentiful, it was much more difficult to keep. To put it another way, without today's preservatives and refrigeration techniques, it was much more difficult to keep food fresh.